Contents

D1473627

Fukuzawa Yûkichi

Fukuzawa Yûkichi and wife Toki Okin, 1900 (used with permission of the Fukuzawa Memorial Center at Keiô University.

Helen M. Hopper

University of Pittsburgh

Fukuzawa Yûkichi

From Samurai to Capitalist

The Library of World Biography

Series Editor: Peter N. Stearns

PEARSON
Longman

New York   Boston   San Francisco
London   Toronto   Sydney   Tokyo   Singapore   Madrid
Mexico City   Munich   Paris   Cape Town   Hong Kong   Montreal

Vice President and Publisher: Priscilla McGeehon
Acquisitions Editor: Erika Gutierrez
Executive Marketing Manager: Sue Westmoreland
Production Coordinator: Shafiena Ghani
Senior Cover Design Manager/Designer: Nancy Danahy
Cover Photo: Used with permission of the Fukuzawa Memorial
    Center at Keiô University
Manufacturing Manager: Mary Fischer
Electronic Page Makeup: Jeffrey Streber
Printer and Binder: RR Donnelley and Sons Company/Harrisonburg
Cover Printer: Coral Graphics Services, Inc.

Library of Congress Cataloging-in-Publication Data

Hopper, Helen M.
    Fukuzawa Yûkichi: from samurai to capitalist / Helen M. Hopper.
        p. cm. -- (Library of world biography)
    Includes bibliographical references and index.
    ISBN 0-321-07802-0
    1. Fukuzawa, Yûkichi, 1835-1901. 2. Japan--Officials and
employees--Biography. 3. Journalists--Japan--Biography. 4. Educators--
Japan--Biography. I. Title. II. Series.

DS884.F8H67 2004
952.03'1'092--dc22
[B]   2004046519

Please visit our website at http://www.ablongman.com

ISBN 0-321-07802-0

1 2 3 4 5 6 7 8 9 10—DOH—07 06 05 04

For Akiko Kiso

Editor's Preface

"Biography is history seen through the prism of a person."

—LOUIS FISCHER

It is often challenging to identify the roles and experiences of individuals in world history. Larger forces predominate. Yet biography provides important access to world history. It shows how individuals helped shape the society around them. Biography also offers concrete illustrations of larger patterns in political and intellectual life, in family life, and in the economy.

The Longman Library of World Biography series seeks to capture the individuality and drama that mark human character. It deals with individuals operating in one of the main periods of world history, while also reflecting issues in the particular society around them. Here, the individual illustrates larger themes of time and place. The interplay between the personal and the general is always the key to using biography in history, and world history is no exception. Always, too, there is the question of personal agency: how much do individuals, even great ones, shape their own lives and environment, and how much are they shaped by the world around them?

PETER N. STEARNS

Author's Preface

Fukuzawa Yûkichi was one of Japan's most farsighted and influential private citizens in the last half of the nineteenth century. He spent the first two decades of his life simply surviving the oppressive and monotonous life of a lower-level *samurai* in a backwater castle town in southern Japan during the feudal period of the Tokugawa administration. Finally he managed to connive his way into a more exciting life. He had determined that the key to future success was Western studies. Therefore, he sought access to Dutch learning at a time when Westerners were isolated to a single small island off Japan's shores. After America and then European nations forced Japan to open its borders, Fukuzawa sought out influential officials to support his application to travel abroad. Once in America and Europe, he carefully observed and recorded the ways in which these westerners had applied advanced science and technology to the acquisition of national wealth and international power. He returned to Japan in the midst of the civil wars of the 1860s. It was a trying time, but also a time filled with the excitement of political, social, and cultural change. A new government was formed in 1868, ruled by an oligarchy in the name of the Emperor Meiji, with the intent of reforming all aspects of Japanese life. Fukuzawa, though a private citizen, contributed greatly to the shape of the new Japan.

Fukuzawa founded his success on two pillars: study based on Western scientific, economic, and political thought and action based on practical experience and the anticipation of public needs. Study and action together with hard work and a keen intuition made it possible for him to position himself as a significant voice in political and foreign policy debates, educational and cultural discussions, and journalistic and business conquests. He was not averse to conniving in order to be present at the important events shaping the new Japan or to taking advantage of personal and professional relationships in a cause he felt was vital to his or the nation's advancement. He was also perfectly willing to change his position on significant issues if it seemed advantageous to do so. For example, in the beginning of the Meiji Period, in the early 1870s, he preached and practiced individualism, freedom, and independence. It was the individual citizen that interested him. National reforms and institutions should support the citizen, especially the educated citizen, and the nuclear family. By the end of the century he had moved firmly into the camp of emperor centered patriotic nationalism at home and imperialism abroad. It was the community—in fact, the nation—that was of greatest importance.

To propagate his ideas, Fukuzawa participated in a variety of arenas of public discourse. He founded a school that prepared young men for influential positions, particularly in the areas of banking, commerce, and business, which continues today as the prestigious *Keiô* University. Meanwhile, he secured a place of honor and respect among the reading public through his published books, both translations of Western writings and his own works, and with his editorials on national debates in *Jiji Shinpô*, the newspaper he founded and owned. He promoted the Western performance of speech making and oral debate, and he used this medium to express his opinions on topics ranging from women's rights to foreign policy. The public was never at a loss to know what Fukuzawa was thinking about an issue of consequence, and those in high places could be sure that he would make his case known to them in private.

Fukuzawa was well known during his lifetime because he involved himself in the major political, economic, and foreign policy decisions of the day. When he wanted a forum, he had a national one. His advice and argument attracted the attention of both the public and those in power, in sum, all who made or read the news or who listened to their compatriots discussing the latest events. When he wanted to stay behind a curtain, he exerted his influence through his ready access to the rich and powerful and his father/son relationship with the many alumni of his school, *Keiô* University. He was powerful, independent, and respected during his lifetime and is still remembered as one of Japan's most outstanding and revered historical figures. He has the status of a god, even among those, or perhaps especially among those, in Japan who know little of the full story of his significance for nineteenth century cultural, political, and economic history.

Fukuzawa was an important intellectual who, like so many influential nineteenth-century Japanese thinkers, intermixed liberal and conservative ideas as he sought a philosophy that encompasses both the moral and practical requirements of a nation stepping onto the world stage for the first time. He did not look for consistency of thought but rather for results from practical action. In spite of his protestations to the contrary, he never completely surrendered his early Confucian training to the new knowledge he embraced from the West. Consequently, as the century wore on, his eclectic thinking became more nationalistic, even chauvinistic, and though he never stopped admiring the West, he wanted Japan to emulate the West in order to equal or exceed Western international power. He achieved wealth, status, and influence well beyond what he could have dreamed of while he lay about in the backward castle town of his youth. After his death in 1901, he was eulogized as one of the greatest figures of Japan's modernizing decades. Mention his name today and Japanese people immediately take on a reverential pose, nodding in agreement over his continued place of exaltation in Japan's pantheon of heroes. The concrete recognition of this awe-inspiring position is his photo on Japan's ten-thousand yen bill, its largest currency denomination. I think he would find this a fitting memorial to his national prominence and his personal accomplishments during the period in which Japan emerged as a modern nation.

Acknowledgments

I have had much help in the research and writing of this biography. My greatest appreciation must go to Professor Norio Tamaki of *Keiô* University, who gave me his insights on Fukuzawa both while he was visiting at the University of Pittsburgh and when I visited him at *Keiô* in Tokyo. His recent book has been invaluable. I would also like to thank Mrs. Akao, librarian at the Fukuzawa Memorial Center at *Keiô* for her help in finding photographs and materials that I could use. On my trip to the old castle town of Nakatsu I was introduced to Mr. Mukumoto, the curator of the Fukuzawa Museum, who discussed Fukuzawa and the Nakatsu domain with me, showed me ancient castle town maps, and gave me photographs. Once again I have Professor Tamaki to thank for this introduction. At the University of Pittsburgh I want to thank our Japanese bibliographer, Sachie Noguchi, who obtained a complete set of the *Jiji Shinpô*, Fukuzawa's newspaper, for the library, in part because of my interest. For assistance at the Ogata Museum in Osaka and an introduction to the old storehouse area of Osaka, I want to thank my friend Mieko Hosomi, a reporter for the *Sankei Shimbun*, the newspaper that grew out of Fukuzawa's *Jiji Shinpô*. While in London in March 2003, I discussed with Leslie Downer the relationship between Fukuzawa Momosuke and his wife, Fukuzawa Yûkichi's daughter, Fusa. This conversation and her book *Madame Sadayakko* gave me insight into another aspect of Fukuzawa's family relations. In Edinburgh in September 2003 I had the great honor to meet Carmen Blacker, who contributed so much to Fukuzawa scholarship. I thank her for several conversations, which broadened my knowledge on this Japanese figure. For several years of personal friendship I thank Akiko Kiso, my host and scholarly inspiration in Japan, and it is to her that I dedicate this book. I express great appreciation to the University of Pittsburgh and the Japan Iron and Steel Foundation and to the Northeast

Regional Conference of the Association for Asian Studies who provided the funding for my research in Japan. Finally, thank you to the many readers who have offered advice along the way: Andrew Hernandez III, Thomas S. Hegarty, Cynthia Jones, John D. Boswell, Greg P. Guelcher, David J. Ulbrich, Robert D. Fiala, Denise Davidson, Bryan Ganaway.

A Note on Names

In accordance with the usual practice, Japanese names in the body of this work appear in the order of family name followed by given name.

HELEN M. HOPPER

Fukuzawa Yûkichi

A Samurai Breaks Free

Fukuzawa House in Nakatsu (Fukuzawa Memorial Museum). (H. Hopper, 2001)

Fukuzawa Yûkichi was born in Osaka on January 10, 1835. His family, members of the Nakatsu-*han*, had been living there for a decade because his father, Fukuzawa Hyakusuke, held the position of overseer of the treasury, or accountant, at the Nakatsu-*han* storehouse situated on one of the many waterways in Osaka. This *kurashiki* housed the *daimyô*'s rice, which was available for exchange after all *samurai* stipends had been paid and the *daimyô* had taken what he needed for his household's consumption. The rice shipped to Osaka, the kitchen city, would be stored until exchanged through merchants or "rice jobbers" for goods and cash. Hyakusuke, a **lower-level** *samurai*, was sent to oversee the *daimyô*'s store since, theoretically, no upper-level *samurai* would stoop so low as to deal with the fourth **class**, the merchants. And yet the *daimyô* needed an official he could trust to mediate with the powerful merchants who bought and sold rice and who loaned money. Someone had to protect the **domain**'s wealth, and it was better that a lower-level *samurai* perform that unpleasant duty. Thus, Hyakusuke and his wife, O-Jun, also of a lower *samurai* family, moved to Osaka in about 1826; and all of their five children, including Yûkichi, the youngest, an older brother, and three older sisters, were born there.

The position in Osaka, though clerical and suitable to a lower *samurai*, was a good one, for it provided some material comforts beyond the basic **stipend**. Duty for any *samurai* at either **Edo** or Osaka meant opportunities for a few spoils of office, at the very least profit from the travel allowance. These distant jobs could also mean opportunity for graft and corruption, which could increase an official's private purse. While Fukuzawa did not put his father in this category, he did comment in an 1877 article that "even those *samurai* whose conduct was upright and blameless found it in practice almost impossible to avoid being caught up in the toils of 'extra emoluments.'" Hyakusuke served a ten-year term in Osaka and then was required to sign on again for two single-year extensions. Each of these gave him a cash bonus. Consequently, it must have been doubly devastating for the family when Hyakusuke died in June 1836, leaving his eleven-year-old elder son as head of the family. Of course, the widow and her five children were forced to return to Nakatsu-*han*, where the family was reduced to living on its small official stipend. The move was especially difficult for the thirty-three-year-old O-Jun, who had learned to enjoy big-city living. In fact, the whole family kept pretty much to themselves in this "backwater" castle town in Kyushu, for their neighbors, and even their relatives, remarked on the family's strange Osaka accent and big-city ways.

The Restricted Life of a Nakatsu Samurai

The *daimyô* of Nakatsu-*han* came from the Okudaira family. It was the Okudaira *daimyô* who had signed an oath of allegiance to Japan's most powerful leader, the **shogun**. Therefore, it was the Okudaira *daimyô* who was responsible for following the rules laid down by the *shogun* and his central government, the **bakufu**, in Edo. As the domain's highest official, the *daimyô* had to make the long trek from Nakatsu to Edo every other year and reside there in a dwelling that he had built at great expense to his domain. His primary duty, however, was to rule over his own vassals, the *samurai*, and the commoners in the **castle town**, as well as the peasants in the villages. It was also the *daimyô*'s obligation to protect and provide for all of the people of his domain during difficult times. The Nakatsu-*han* had a population of about 80,000. Of these about 80 percent or more lived in villages and produced the 100,000 **koku** of rice stipulated in surveys completed about two hundred years earlier. In fact, the actual amount of rice produced varied year by year, but it always provided a good living for the *daimyô* and his family and for the upper *samurai*. It provided a much more restricted living for lower *samurai* and the peasants who actually cultivated the crop.

The *samurai* formed the small group at the top of a pyramid of classes which had been fixed by law for over two hundred years. Since rice was so important to the survival of the society, the peasants who grew it formed the second class within the hierarchy. Status within this group varied according to a family's political and social role within a village. Because both the *samurai* in the castle towns and the peasants in the villages had great need for every sort of product and service, from farm tools to swords to clothing to buildings, the artisans made up the third class. They gained differentiated status based on their skill and usefulness. Products might include *samurai* swords, temple bells, tools, stoves, horseshoes, and pottery. Services ranged from thatching roofs to making **tatami** for flooring and building frames for dwellings. The fourth class was composed of merchants. This lowest designation derived from Confucian thinking, which taught that handling money or participating in any business operations was defiling. It was certainly not something that a *samurai* should indulge in. Fukuzawa Yûkichi was often told that his father objected to his brother and sisters being taught any form of calculation, even abstract notions of mathematics, for this was demeaning to even those of lower *samurai* status. Once when Fukuzawa Hyakusuke discovered that a teacher to whom he had sent his older children was testing them in times tables, he exclaimed that "it was abominable that innocent children should be taught to use numbers—the tool of merchants." Late in life when Yûkichi told this story he must have chuckled as he thought of his own long success as an entrepreneur and his influence within financial circles.

Fukuzawa Yûkichi described the *samurai*'s economic situation in an article he wrote about the **han** in 1877 and in his autobiography, written in 1899. He reported that there were 1500 *samurai* in Nakatsu-*han*, who "were divided broadly into two classes, though in all there were as many as a hundred different minute distinctions between their social positions and official duties." The differences between the two major ranks could be immediately observed by walking through the town area around the castle or by looking at a **Tokugawa** era map. Upper *samurai* all lived close to the castle. Surprisingly, even merchants, the lowest class in the four primary divisions, lived closer than lower *samurai*, who were furthest away and to the east of the castle. Fukuzawa's family was one of the *samurai* families most distant of all from the castle. This can still be observed today by walking the area from the castle to Fukuzawa's house, which has been preserved. Of the 1500 men "permitted to wear the sword," which marked them as *samurai*, about 400 were upper *samurai*, and the rest were lower like Fukuzawa's own father.

Yûkichi lamented that lower-ranking *samurai* received such a small annual stipend that they and their wives and older children were forced to take on side jobs to simply survive. Such jobs could include making straw sandals, raising crickets and weaving cricket cages, twisting threads or paper to make hair ties, making umbrellas, growing and potting flowers, making wooden clogs (**geta**), selling bamboo shoots or other foodstuffs, making and selling carvings or other artworks—in other words, participating in any small endeavor that might turn a small profit. Perhaps the most important side job for the family's livelihood was the wife's work spinning thread and weaving cotton cloth, both to clothe her family and to be used as exchange items for cash or other necessities. Of course, all of this made a mockery of the *samurai*'s insistence that he was above the trading and money exchange that marked the lower-class merchant. Tokugawa laws might categorize people strictly by birth, but necessity was stretching and altering these categories according to actual circumstances even while the laws remained static.

The poverty Fukuzawa described was a lifelong circumstance. Lower-level *samurai* could never advance beyond the highest designation of their status category. Regardless of talent or ability, even the lowest rung of the upper *samurai* ranks was beyond the reach of Yûkichi and his cohorts. This meant that, since the Fukuzawa family had already attained the highest status within their rank, neither those living, nor any of their descendents could expect to ever advance further. As Fukuzawa said, there was about as great a possibility for promotion from his rank to a higher level "as a four-legged beast [might] hope to fly like a bird." Given this rigidity within the system, Fukuzawa's father was quite fortunate to have had the position of overseer at the *daimyô*'s storehouse in Osaka.

The *daimyô* and the four hundred upper-level *samurai* lived quite well. Even during the most difficult times during the mid-nineteenth century, the final decades of Tokugawa rule, these wealthy *samurai* from Nakatsu continued to live comfortably, though not without accumulating debt. Fukuzawa explained that each upper *samurai* had a paper fief that provided a gross stipend of between 100-250 *koku* of rice. This worked out to considerably less in actual receipts, perhaps 22 to 60 *koku*. (That is perhaps a little low given the usual rate of 60 percent for the cultivators and 40 percent for the *samurai*, but it makes the point.) Though this does not seem very lucrative, compared with Fukuzawa's father's stipend of about fourteen *koku* with a net income of about eight *koku*, it was enormous. Fukuzawa Hyakusuke had to feed, clothe and house two adults and five children on his income. Using the rule of thumb of one *koku* (about five bushels) per adult for a year's consumption, there was little rice left over to be traded or converted to cash to provide for the many other needs such as oil, vegetables, salt, paper, clothing, and household goods. One must keep in mind, as well, that the *bakufu* had proclaimed primogeniture the inheritance law of the land. That meant the *samurai* stipend could be inherited only by the eldest son. At birth Yûkichi could not expect to see any of the stipend after he attained adulthood, as it would accrue to his elder brother. His options were to be adopted by a family that did not have a son, become a priest, or remain at home, paying for his keep through odd jobs. The three sisters would, it was hoped, marry an eldest son or, if they remained at home, would work to bring in additional income.

There were significant social as well as economic differences between the Fukuzawa family and the four hundred *samurai* and their families in the upper level. The language of the upper classes showed their superiority, and the forms of address required of the lower-level *samurai*, their inferiority. It wasn't simply a matter of learning correct usage and thereby appearing cultured and educated. Lower-class *samurai* were simply not permitted to use the language of the upper classes. The lowest level *samurai*, those even below the Fukuzawa family, had to prostrate themselves, falling to the ground, upon meeting an upper class *samurai*. Every movement, action, activity, interaction reflected a *samurai*'s status. The use of the written language reflected the differences of status; the manner of arriving and leaving a house exhibited the status differences; what rooms one was received in clearly reflected ranking; and lower *samurai* walked while those in the upper class rode horses. One of the most significant differences involved which *samurai* could be granted an audience with those of the highest status.

Both of Yûkichi's parents came from the lower ranks, as would be expected, since it was forbidden for the two primary divisions to intermarry. Theoretically *samurai* could only marry within their own ranks. By the nineteenth century this meant there were few enough candidates for a *samurai* hoping to marry someone from Nakatsu and almost as few potential partners from nearby domains. Fukuzawa's father's marriage had been arranged by his family in the early 1820s and by 1826 he had brought his new wife to Osaka with him. Their marriage, therefore, had followed the ideal pattern for a lower-level *samurai*. However, given the poverty characteristic of lower-ranking *samurai* in general, and the fact that they constituted such a small percentage of the total population of a domain, many *samurai*, most especially those of lower status, had begun to marry into merchant families. This was seen as an opportunity for the *samurai* to raise his standard of living and for the merchant family to gain apparent status. Obviously the rigidity of the *bakufu* laws was beginning to crack. Such crossing of absolute class boundaries also meant that women who could not find an eldest, inheriting *samurai* son to marry might have a chance for some sort of marriage outside of her class. Times were definitely in flux.

One inequality that particularly angered Fukuzawa Yûkichi was the inferiority of the education of the lower *samurai* compared with his superiors. It is not surprising, then, that his own education, as well as that of his fellow countrymen, became a primary focus for Fukuzawa. In part the upper classes were better educated because they had the money and leisure to devote to study. As Fukuzawa explained in 1877, "The [upper *samurai*] would read the Confucian Classics and the Books of History, study military strategy, practise horsemanship, spearmanship and swordsmanship, and generally indulge in all the branches of art and learning which were considered at the time to be cultured and noble. Thus their manners were naturally elegant and aristocratic, and many of them could be considered most cultured and refined gentlemen." Lower *samurai*, by contrast, progressed only modestly in classical studies and were primarily instructed in writing and arithmetic. As we have seen, Fukuzawa's father decried the study of arithmetic as a tool of the merchant class. But as Yûkichi noted, lower *samurai* could only hope for offices as minor bureaucrats, and these required clerical abilities, including working with numbers and writing reports and letters. His protesting father's own career attested to this. Although all schooling included calligraphy, upper *samurai* used a more cultured Chinese style of artful writing, while lower were taught a style considered vulgar.

Fukuzawa also wrote of the differences in customs and manners between upper and lower *samurai*. Many of these grew out of the economic discrepancies and the social regulations, but some were based on the traditional image of the *samurai* as a disciple of a military code of honor. Only upper *samurai* could really afford to maintain these fictions in a time of peace and inadequate employment. An upper level *samurai* employed servants so that no one in his household would ever have to travel alone to make purchases. When he did go out, he wore his two swords, which identified him as a *samurai*. Should he need to make purchases, he never carried them home personally, but rather his accompanying servant walked behind him with bundles wrapped up in a *furoshiki* (carrying cloth). Many nineteenth century woodcut pictures illustrate such scenes. At parties upper *samurai* remained stiff and stuffy. Lower *samurai* were quite the opposite. "In short, the manners of the upper *samurai* were elegant and restrained, while those of the lower *samurai* were more rustic and lively." As a consequence, Fukuzawa concluded in his 1877 description of domain life, while Nakatsu-*han samurai* did not dispute the roles they were given, when the Tokugawa were no longer in control, and the rigid *bakufu* rules were overthrown, it was the lower *samurai* who were more capable of adjusting to the new society. He would certainly prove that to be correct in his case.

Breaking Out of Nakatsu

As a lower *samurai*, Fukuzawa was not required to study anything. In fact, he wasn't encouraged to become educated at all. Consequently, it wasn't until he was fourteen that he decided on his own to seek an education. As he put it, "I found that many of the boys of my age were studying these classics; and I became ashamed of myself and willingly started to school." In the beginning he found the study of the books on Chinese philosophy quite difficult but soon he was the one who led discussions and won debates. In addition to the schoolwork, he "was very clever" with his hands and was always inventing and fixing things. This ability came in handy in his impoverished household, as he could make and mend household goods, and he was able to earn extra money by making *geta* and preparing swords.

Soon after beginning his formal education, he outstripped those around him, at least in his own view, and consequently, he felt no need to be obedient to either the gods or to his feudal overlords. His mother, whom he loved and admired greatly, was quite liberal with him and encouraged him to follow his own desires. Since she did not have a strong belief in Buddhism, she did not object to her son's religious waywardness. She told him stories about the family's Osaka days, which led Yûkichi to believe that his father hated the **feudal system** and would have approved of his son's conclusion that his fellow *samurai* exhibited a despotic and arrogant nature. Although Yûkichi did not have any memory of his birth city, Osaka, through his mother's stories he compared his backwater castle town unfavorably with that thriving city and became dissatisfied living in Nakatsu. He found it too provincial and he longed to leave. As the younger son, Yûkichi could not become head of the Fukuzawa family, and so at an early age his mother had arranged for an uncle who had no sons to adopt him. While he awaited coming into this inheritance, Yûkichi decided, in February 1854, that he would leave Nakatsu. At the age of nineteen, therefore, he undertook to further his education elsewhere toward his goal of becoming "the richest man in Japan." Given his social status, one would think he would find it difficult to accomplish the former and impossible to achieve the latter.

When his elder brother set forth on business to Nagasaki, on the opposite coast of Kyushu, Yûkichi jumped at the chance to accompany him. Because the Nakatsu *daimyô* was responsible for management of *bakufu* lands and lower *samurai* like Yûkichi's brother were clerks for the *han*, it is not surprising that Fukuzawa Sannosuke would have business in the *bakufu* controlled city of Nagasaki. This port city was one of Japan's most important centers for commerce, foreign trade, and foreign relations. Even though it was situated within the province of Hizen and thus surrounded by the lands of the powerful Nabeshima family, an historical opponent of the Tokugawa, it had been a primary seat of *bakufu* power since the early 17th century. At that time the Tokugawa *shoguns* eliminated Portuguese trade, prohibited Christianity, which had been a side product of that trade, and resettled the Dutch and Chinese traders at Nagasaki. Finally, the Tokugawa established a policy of *sakoku*, or a closed country, so that it could control foreign intrusion and commerce. At the same time, the *bakufu* actually increased the amount of foreign trade in Japan by providing this access for Dutch and Chinese traders, while controlling unwanted foreign influences.

Yūkichi had heard much of Nagasaki and the Western ambience that enveloped that commercial city. He saw his trip as one of adventure and education with the important corollary of getting away from his confining, backward *han*. Nagasaki was a port city on the other side of the mountains, to the southwest of Nakatsu, but still in the northern half of Kyushu. Just off Nagasaki was the man-made island of **Deshima**, where the Dutch were permitted to bring a ship in each year for purposes of trade. They were also allowed to maintain an enclave on the island. Although the Japanese in Nagasaki could not communicate directly with these foreigners, the excitement of Western technology and scientific know-how was all about. Dutch books were thought to hold the key to knowledge that was beyond the reach of those who knew only the Japanese language. Also, Nagasaki was a center for learning about modern weaponry, a subject that the coastal *han* would need to learn from the West if they were going to prevent the intrusion of unwanted Western ships into Japanese territory.

Yūkichi was determined, then, to study both the Dutch language and the manufacture and technical operation of guns and cannon. He was placed in the home of a *bakufu* official by Okudaira Iki, a member of the Nakatsu *daimyô*'s family. Although Fukuzawa received free room and board with no obligation to work, he did odd jobs, read scholarly works to his benefactor, made copies of books on gunnery for him, and tutored his "not very bright" son. After just two or three months in Nagasaki, he felt he had made good progress learning Dutch, and at the end of a year he felt confident about both his new language facility and his acquisition of the technical intricacies of gunnery.

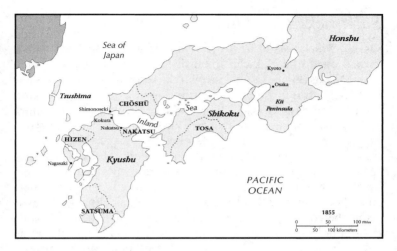

Fukuzawa breaks free–Nakatsu to Osaka, 1855.

Unfortunately, Yûkichi did so well in his studies that he outshone his patron, Okudaira Iki, with the result that this superior contrived to get rid of his competition. A letter was written claiming that Yûkichi's mother was ill and that he would have to return home immediately. The ruse was obvious and, while appearing to leave for Nakatsu, Yûkichi ignored the summons and set off for Edo, the central government's capital, sending his sympathetic mother a letter explaining his plans. There was no possibility that Fukuzawa could continue his education if he returned to Nakatsu; he felt he must break free. Given the internal and external pressures at this time on the delicately balanced *bakufu* (central) -*han* (domainal) system of government, one lower *samurai* breaking the rules would not even be noticed. And so Fukuzawa began his trek east to the capital by foot and by boat, determined to carry out a personal revolt against the feudal system. In this he foreshadowed other lower *samurai* in larger and more aggressive domains who would carry out large-scale revolts that would result in the overthrow of the Tokugawa *bakufu* within fifteen years.

Sidetracked in Osaka

Osaka, which was to be just the first part of a journey to Edo, turned out to be Yûkichi's final destination. The stressful trip from Nagasaki to Osaka in March 1855 was accomplished with very little in the way of either money or belongings and took fifteen days. Yûkichi first walked to Kokura to the north of Nakatsu, making sure that he skirted his own domain so as not to alert the officials to his plans of escape. Within three days, he managed to get a ferry from Kokura across the Straits to Shimonoseki. He then purchased a ride on a crowded boat operated by one of the inexperienced peasants who navigated small boats on the Inland Sea as a profitable sideline. Fukuzawa remembered that the passengers included "all kinds of travelers—a foolish-looking son of a rich man; a bald-headed grandsire; some *geisha*, gay and richly dressed, and other women of questionable reputation; farmers; priests; rich and poor; all sorts, crowded together in the narrow boat, drinking, gambling, clamoring over any nonsensical matter. Among them sat I, forlorn and quiet, like a priest doing penance." The voyage was so unpleasant that Fukuzawa got off thirty-eight miles before Osaka and walked the rest of the way to his *daimyô*'s storehouse, where his brother, Sannosuke, had assumed their father's job as storehouse manager. Once Yûkichi arrived there, his brother, the head of the Fukuzawa household, insisted that Yûkichi should stay, assuring him that he could find competent instruction in Dutch in Osaka. Given the relative positions of the two brothers, Yûkichi had no option but to obey.

Osaka was one of the three largest and most significant cities in Tokugawa-era Japan. Edo, the capital of the Tokugawa *bakufu*, was Japan's political center. Because of the law requiring all *daimyô* to have a permanent presence and at least one residence in Edo, and to be in attendance every other year, Edo had by far the largest number of *samurai* of any city. Like all the other large domains, it, too, had a castle for the *shogun* and his entourage. It also had a large component of merchants, artisans, and other commoners. In the nineteenth century the population was over one million, making Edo the largest city in the world. The imperial city, Kyoto, also one of the three primary cities, was home to the emperor and his courtiers. About one hundred *daimyô* of the approximately 250 *daimyô* throughout the country also maintained a presence, including expensive residences in this city of about four hundred thousand inhabitants. Kyoto was both the cultural hub, with its religious centers and long history of art and literature, and an industrial center with heavily concentrated commerce in textiles supported by many professional weavers. There were also many other successful enterprises. Osaka was known as the "kitchen" city, for it was the commercial heart of Tokugawa Japan. Although it had fallen somewhat on hard times during the nineteenth century, at mid-century it still had over three hundred thousand residents, representing a drop of about one hundred thousand from its most populous period in the mid-eighteenth century.

Osaka was a port city and the final destination of three primary sea routes on which ships transported rice and myriad other products for exchange and sale in this commercial center. One route hugged the entire length of the coast of Honshu on the Japan Sea side, continued around the end of this main island, through the Shimonoseki Strait at the tip of Kyushu, then through the Inland Sea, to the port of Osaka. Another came from northern Honshu and down the Pacific Coast to Edo. The third route continued from Edo, on around the Kii Peninsula and entered the Inland Sea very close to the port of Osaka. In addition, the Yodo River ran between Osaka and Kyoto. It is no wonder that Osaka became a center for successful merchants.

As we have seen, the Fukuzawa household head held the position of overseer of the *daimyô*'s *kurashiki*, or storehouse. This warehouse was situated on the Dôjima River, one of the several rivers that, along with many canals, had access to the port for shipping purposes. Lower *samurai* from other domains also had similar storehouses from which they would transact business with the help of "rice jobbers" and merchants. Compared with Edo, however, there were very few *samurai* in Osaka, while, on the other hand, there were many times more merchants, who exchanged rice for currency and traded all sorts of goods from lacquerware to cotton to dried fish and sardines. Here could be found a market for medicines, incense sticks, bamboo poles, rapeseed oil, folding fans, iron anchors for boats, lumber, altars for festivals, copper for export, and all other products grown, manufactured, extracted from the land, or caught from the sea. And, as the nineteenth century progressed, merchants who were money-lenders had become, perhaps, the most prosperous and privileged of all of that lowly "fourth class" in the official *bakufu* hierarchy.

In addition to the few *samurai*, the large contingent of merchants, and the many artisans who made household goods, constructed buildings and cast iron stoves, wove *tatami* mats, and so forth, there were commoners who provided services. These included unclassified members of society such as doctors, firemen, priests and temple guardians, and city commissioners, all respected professionals necessary to the smooth running of this complex city. There were also what some scholars call "backstreet tenants" who were poor, often without permanent employment, who lived in the alleyways behind the primary streets of the various wards that made up the large city. Osaka, like all other castle towns, large and small, included the homeless and the day workers, whose status was substantially below the four official classes. Finally, at the very bottom of the scale were the outcasts, the handlers of meat and leather and people who cleaned up after executions and did other defiling jobs according to Buddhist thought, and the itinerant entertainers, such as jugglers, street musicians, and travelling actors.

Joining the Tekijuku, a School for Dutch Studies

True to his promise, Sannosuke found a school in Osaka at which his brother could continue his Dutch studies. This was the famous *Tekijuku* run by the medical doctor and Dutch studies scholar, Ogata Kôan. Recognizing the importance of trade and commerce in Osaka, Ogata established his school very close to where the domains' *kurashiki* stood on the rivers and canals at the heart of merchant activity. The building, with its kitchen; interior garden; private rooms for the *sensei*, his wife, and nine children; and rooms upstairs for the students, stands today as it did when Fukuzawa attended the school. The wooden, two story structure, a typical nineteenth-century merchant style house, situated on the Tosabori Canal, was bought by Ogata in 1843. Currently it is surrounded by tall concrete and steel office buildings in one of Osaka's primary business sections. Office workers eat lunch in the garden outside by the statue of Ogata Kôan, who remains a well-known historical figure in contemporary Osaka.

Ogata founded his school in 1838 and remained as its head until he was summoned to Edo in 1862 to establish a school there and to become the Tokugawa *shogun*'s personal physician. He died there, suddenly, one year later. From the Tekijuku's inception, most students at the school expected to become medical doctors. They came to the school from near and far to study Dutch language and Dutch medical texts with Ogata, who was already a prominent Western-style physician and scholar in his own right. Using Dutch language translations of German texts, he translated into Japanese the latest in scientific and medical scholarship. He wrote his own medical treatises, as well. In the 1850s he promoted vaccination for smallpox and worked to convince physicians and government officials to establish vaccination stations to help eliminate this devastating disease. In 1858, following a cholera epidemic, he wrote an article entitled "The Standard Methods of Cholera Treatment." As a practical application of that research, he set up a cholera vaccination station with the help of wealthy neighborhood merchants. Ogata used a Dutch-Japanese dictionary to translate European scholarship for himself and his students, as well as teaching physics, chemistry, and medicine directly from Dutch books. In this way he brought Western scientific and technical knowledge to his students and his community. Although Fukuzawa was perhaps his most renowned student, Ogata also trained others from different domains who distinguished themselves in medicine. In addition, several of his students became political advocates for and against the Tokugawa regime in the 1860s, the stormy final decade of *bakufu* rule.

Sannosuke could be proud of his arrangement for Yûkichi when the younger brother was admitted to the Tekijuku in April of 1855. Because the school was only a ten-minute walk from his brother's Nakatsu-*han* residence in Osaka, Yûkichi entered as a day student. Unfortunately, this first experience as a student of Dutch studies ended by the summer of 1856, when he was forced to return to Nakatsu with his very ill brother. Sannosuke died that fall at the age of 30. Due to this sad turn of events, Yûkichi was forced to revoke his earlier agreement of adoption by an uncle and, at the age 21, to become head of the Fukuzawa family. Reluctantly he settled down to the boring and inhibiting life of a lower-level *samurai*, an existence that he thought he had escaped.

As household head, Yûkichi was required to take his turn at guard duty at the castle and do whatever else his lord, the *daimyô*, might demand. This tiresome existence in the town he hated lasted, fortunately, only about three months. By December 1856 he had obtained permission from the *daimyô* to return to the Tekijuku in Osaka, this time to study military weaponry. Although this might seem a strange subject for Ogata's school, because the Tekijuku specialized in Western science and technology, gunnery was assumed to be included in the curriculum by officials in Nakatsu. As an advisor told Yûkichi, an application to study "Dutch learning" would not be accepted, for there was no precedent for it, but there was precedent for weaponry study. "It doesn't matter whether your statement is true to fact or not. It has to be gunnery." The advice was accepted and permission was granted. Yûkichi was concerned about leaving his much-beloved mother, who would have only Sunnosuke's daughter to keep her company, since her own three daughters had already married and begun families of their own. However, his mother assured her son that he would have her blessing wherever he went and in whatever he chose to do. Yûkichi appreciated the unconditional support his mother so freely gave him. He never forgot the debt he owed her. While she remained in Nakatsu, he sent her money and took every opportunity to return home for brief periods to see her. Later, when he was settled and financially able, he brought her to live with his family in Tokyo.

When he returned to the Tekijuku in the winter of 1857, Yûkichi entered as a boarder. He joined the other students on the second floor of Ogata's building. There he laid down his bedding and arranged his belongings on one mat (a 6-foot-by-3-foot *tatami* area) in the ten-mat dormitory room. This would constitute his living space for two years. The upper floor also included a small room, which contained the library of ten printed Dutch books and additional hand-copied ones, and the largest room in the building (about 32 mats), which served as a classroom. The curriculum was set by Ogata and drew from the Dutch language books on medicine and physics that he had obtained and other Western scientific studies hand-copied in Dutch. All students began with the 6,000-page Dutch/Japanese dictionary and the requirement to quickly absorb this and then proceed to translate and interpret the books from the library in a prescribed order. Yûkichi, who had a head start given his study in Nagasaki and his previous year as a day-student, progressed very quickly and soon became a senior student, a member of the top, or eighth, grade, and then head student for the entire school. In both his official positions he received a much-needed stipend and gained experience as a teacher. The famous *sensei*, Ogata, in fact did not do much teaching, though on particular occasions he was requested by the senior students to lecture to them. Yûkichi remembered how impressed he was "by the minuteness of his (Ogata's) observations, and at the same time by the boldness of his conclusions." The student/teacher further observed that "both in reputation and in actual accomplishment Ogata-*sensei* was a foremost scholar of his time in the new Western studies."

Although the students worked hard and followed a schedule that left little opportunity for sleep, they did manage to find time to carouse about the cheaper, less-desirable Osaka neighborhoods, or, when really penniless, to buy a bottle of sake to share in their room. Fukuzawa remarked often throughout his later life what a heavy drinker he was in those days (though he claimed that he usually confined such offensive behavior to post-examination periods). Besides drinking, a primary entertainment for the students, when resources permitted, was eating out. Two beef-stands were favorites even though, he admitted, it was impossible to tell whether the strong-smelling, tough meat was from a cow that had been slaughtered or one that had simply died. One of these beef-stands "was near Naniwa Bridge, and the other near the prostitute quarters of Shinmachi—the lowest sort of eating places. No ordinary man ever entered them. All their customers were *gorotsuki*, or city bullies, who exhibited their fully tattooed torsos, and the students of Ogata's school," Fukuzawa explained in his autobiography.

Most of the time, however, Fukuzawa and his classmates studied. And though it would seem that their study consisted simply of copying pages and pages of Dutch text rather than actually absorbing ideas, in fact, they also had to explicate the meaning of the texts during pressured arguments, which served as examinations. Students progressed through eight grades, with about eight to ten day–and boarding students in each grade. No student moved to a higher grade until his recitation was graded satisfactory. In later years Fukuzawa bragged about the rigorous standards of this Osaka school, remembering that as a student he firmly believed that the Osaka Dutch education was superior to that provided in the capital at Edo. Furthermore, he and the other students constantly rated Dutch studies, in general, higher than Chinese studies, especially Chinese medicine. Fukuzawa confessed in his autobiography that "by hating Chinese medicine so thoroughly, we came to dislike everything which had any connection with Chinese culture. Our general opinion was that we should rid our country of the influences of the Chinese altogether." This attitude did not fade for, as we shall see, anti-Chinese feeling colored Fukuzawa's perspective toward Japan's international policies, especially at the time of the Sino-Japanese War in the last decade of the century.

In hindsight, then, Fukuzawa rated his Western studies over his earlier Chinese and Japanese historical and philosophical learning. The scholar Tetsuo Najita contends that Fukuzawa overstates both the supremacy of Western learning in his education and the exclusive influence of Western ideas in his thinking. Fukuzawa had studied Chinese classics through Japanese and Chinese scholarly writing on *Confucianism*, Buddhism, and *Neo-Confucianism*. Professor Najita, then, has traced Fukuzawa's intellectual roots to, among others, an eighteenth century thinker who emphasized the study of mathematics and strongly favored translation of Western scientific writings. Fukuzawa, though eclectic in his educational background, tended in later years to attribute his ideas to only Western sources. As confirmation that native thinking had, in fact, been internalized, Professor Najita refers us to Fukuzawa's own speeches given during the last quarter of the century, which reflected his earlier education.

Such intertwining of Japanese learning with Western learning would have been approved by Fukuzawa's *sensei*, Ogata, who had said that no one should even begin Western studies until the age of twenty-one and then only after mastering the principles of Tokugawa Confucian thought. It is not surprising, however, that in his 1899 autobiography Fukuzawa credited Western thought alone as the foundation of his ideas. After all, his fame and success grew out of his perpetuation of the theme of "Western enlightenment," which motivated much of Japan's modernization. Fukuzawa saw himself at the forefront of this movement. He proclaimed in his autobiography that Osaka trained the best scholars, in general, and that of these he was, indeed, the very best. And so it was necessary to bury, in name if not in fact, the role that earlier study of Chinese and Japanese texts played in his education, for he had a vested interest in keeping his philosophical and educational lineage pure.

In 1858 leaders of the Nakatsu-*han* residing in Edo heard about the student Fukuzawa Yûkichi, a member of their own domain, who had distinguished himself at the well-known Osaka Tekijuku. Fukuzawa was immediately summoned to Edo to become the new head of the Nakatsu-*han* **Dutch studies** school. Fukuzawa agreed to the move with great enthusiasm, and after returning briefly to Nakatsu to bid his mother farewell once again, he left Osaka to begin a new adventure. The stipend he was to receive for teaching was almost as much again as his *samurai* allotment as head of the Fukuzawa family. In addition, he received other benefits, including money for a servant, a role that he gave to one of his friends from the Tekijuku. Fukuzawa, his "servant," and another Tekijuku classmate set out together on the three-hundred-mile journey from Osaka to Edo to begin a new life in the Tokugawa *bakufu*'s capital.

The Lure of the West

Fukuzawa Yûkichi arrived in Edo during a time of national upheaval caused in part by international intrusion. By the fall of 1858, both *bakufu* politics and commerce had succumbed to the power of American foreign policy. Consequently, when Fukuzawa arrived to take up his position as head of the Nakatsu-*han* school for Dutch studies, he discovered a new foreign influence that would change both his own approach to Western learning and his school's curriculum. He soon realized that the Western studies in Dutch were out of date; English was the new key to modern education.

Within the first few months after arriving in Edo, Fukuzawa decided to visit the foreign enclave in the village of Yokohama, southwest of Edo, to test out his Dutch. Upon his arrival in that treaty port, he found to his surprise that he could not communicate with anyone. In fact, he couldn't even identify what language the foreigners were speaking. As he wrote in his autobiography, "I had been striving with all my powers for many years to learn the Dutch language. And now when I had reason to believe myself one of the best in the country, I found that I could not even read the signs of merchants who had come to trade with us from foreign lands." Dismayed but determined, Fukuzawa bought a two-volume book on English conversation and returned home. By that time he had walked "for twenty-four hours, a distance of some fifty miles, going and coming.

"But," he recalled, "the fatigue of my legs was nothing compared with the bitter disappointment in my heart." Not one to dwell on failure, however, he began the study of English immediately, working with his English conversation books and a Dutch-English dictionary. He would conquer this unanticipated obstacle and would make the English language and the new Western learning the foundation of his future success.

Intrusion From the West

In 1837, not long after Fukuzawa's birth, the American ship the *Morrison*, which was based in Canton, China, sailed from Macao to Japan with two Americans, a businessman and a missionary, masterminding the voyage. They brought with them seven Japanese castaways who had left their homeland illegally. The American instigators believed that having these natives on board would ensure that their ship would be welcomed in Edo Bay. This was not to be. The *bakufu*, fearful that foreign intruders would force themselves on Japan in the same manner that they had overrun neighboring China, fired on the *Morrison* with the few mortars at hand. Later, when the ship tried to land at Kagoshima on the tip of Kyushu, the *daimyō* of Satsuma-*han* greeted the interlopers in the same unfriendly manner. Many officials, however, both in the *bakufu* and the coastal domains, recognized that they would be no match for an invasion of greater strength, and they began to worry about forced intrusion from the West. Indeed, they had cause to be concerned. When the angered Americans of the *Morrison* returned to China, they sent a message home demanding that the United States government organize an expedition of warships, which would carry an ultimatum to Japan to permit international commerce and treat shipwrecked sailors in a civilized manner or suffer severe consequences.

In fact, for the time being, the *bakufu* heard no more from America on this issue. Just the same, *bakufu* officials could envision the specter of foreign intrusion on the horizon. They watched in fear as the Chinese fought and lost the Opium War of 1839-42 to the British. It was only too obvious that the weak

Chinese had suffered from inadequate military preparedness and inferior technology and firepower. News of the unfavorable terms of the Treaty of 1842 traveled quickly to Japan's shores. Most worrying for the *bakufu* were the stipulations that China must open five coastal cities as **treaty ports** with special rights for British nationals, who would be permitted to reside there. The *bakufu* realistically concluded that Britain would soon be knocking at their door. The government was right about a forthcoming intrusion but wrong about which country would pressure Japan first.

Just six months before Fukuzawa Yûkichi left Nakatsu for Nagasaki to begin Dutch studies, Japan was jolted by naval intrusion from a different part of the West, the United States of America. On July 8, 1853, Commodore Matthew Calbraith Perry sailed past the town of Shimoda at the tip of the Izu Peninsula and into the Uraga Channel, which led to Edo Bay and the main port of the Tokugawa capital. This was a terrifying, if not totally unexpected, penetration by a Western power into the very heart of the political power of Japan. Although not evident at the time, this event signaled the end of Japan's two-hundred-year period of carefully controlled foreign trade. The ensuing international confrontation would also provide personal advantages for Fukuzawa, who within the next few years would eagerly seize opportunities to travel to America and Europe and would intensify his study of English as well as Western culture and science.

Perry's "Black Ships"

By 1853 the United States had achieved military and diplomatic successes, which directed the government's attention toward the Western seaboard of the continent and then further west across the Pacific Ocean to the Far East. In June 1846, the Congress had approved the 49th parallel as the final northern U.S. border for the the Oregon Territory, thus resolving a major dispute with Great Britain without resorting to war. A month before, however, the same Congress voted overwhelmingly to declare war on Mexico. This war was finally concluded in February

1848, with the Treaty of Guadalupe Hidalgo, which gave the U.S. territory extending its borders to the Pacific. By 1849, Americans were headed in great numbers to the goldfields of California, and flotillas of sailing ships were discovering the advantages of Western ports as they sailed from the East Coast around the tip of South America, bringing men and supplies to exploit the new wealth of America's West Coast. The doctrine of the 1840s, which proclaimed that America had a "**manifest destiny**" to spread out and possess the whole of the continent had been achieved. Now a new "manifest destiny" appeared in the offing through commercial expansion across the Pacific to the Far East.

It was amid this climate that in 1851 Secretary of State Daniel Webster convinced President Millard Fillmore to finance an expedition to force open ports in Japan to achieve the new American "manifest destiny." It was also Webster who convinced Matthew Calbraith Perry, a successful and renowned naval officer, to take command of this operation. It took some time to outfit the ships and launch the expedition. By the time Perry sailed into Edo Bay, Webster was dead and Fillmore had been replaced by Franklin Pierce as president. The journey, begun in November of 1852, followed the traditional route from the East Coast around the tip of Africa, through the Indian Ocean to the Malaccan Straits and Singapore and then on to China. After briefly calling at ports in China, Macao, and Hong Kong, Perry sailed on to Okinawa in the Ryûkyû Islands. Finally, on July 8, 1853, after seven months on the high seas and in foreign ports, his four ships, including two sailing vessels, the *Plymouth* and the *Saratoga*, and two of the new type of steam-driven ships, the *Susquehanna* and the *Mississippi*, dropped anchor in the Uraga Channel, which led into Edo Bay. It was the latter two warships that intrigued and frightened the Japanese, for they belched black smoke from stacks in the middle of the ships. This phenomenon accounted for the name "Black Ships," which was to be given Perry's squadron, and the obsession with memorializing these immense and powerful warships in woodblock prints and drawings for years to come.

Perry had been given a letter addressed to his "Great and Good Friend, the Emperor of Japan," which had been drafted by Webster and signed by President Fillmore. The goal of the U.S. government was quite modest, from its point of view, emphasizing the importance of providing coaling stations for ships at sea, treating shipwrecked sailors humanely and returning them to their land of origin, and permitting commercial ventures between the U.S. and Japan. As Webster had put it, this was the opportunity for American merchants to forge the "last link in that great chain, which unites all nations of the world." It was indeed the final piece in the fabric that was America's "manifest destiny." Perry's expedition, then, seemed a logical and appropriate step for the new naval power that was the United States. For Japan's leaders, both at the *bakufu* and the *han* levels, this display of foreign power was terrifying. For the ordinary Japanese, who watched the ships come through the channel, the "burning ships on the horizon" were an awesome sight, which created "a great hubbub," a "great uproar," and considerable "confusion."

After much military posturing on both sides during the four days that followed dropping anchor, it was decided that Perry could present his letters to appropriate Tokugawa officials on July 14. Accompanied by 250 armed sailors, Perry, in full dress uniform with sword and colt revolver at his side, was rowed ashore. He was greeted by elaborately dressed Japanese officials in the finest traditional formal court clothing of silk and brocade. The letters were presented, and the Americans' formal commentary was translated into Dutch and then into Japanese. The primary import of these remarks was that Perry and his entourage would be back for an answer to America's requirements by the spring of 1854 and would, at that time, appear with a larger squadron of ships. Three days later, after progressing further up the Uraga Channel and making further soundings and mappings for their return, the Americans pulled up anchor and set off again for Okinawa, China, and, finally, Macao. The extent of the upheaval that these ten days had created in a Japanese *bakufu* already in considerable disarray was greater than any of the Americans involved could have imagined.

A Stunned Bakufu Seeks Advice

The *bakufu* had not been without warning of the American expedition. They had received information from the Dutch in Nagasaki, who had been approached by the Americans for maps of Japan. The *shogun* and his highest officials, however, either refused to believe the information they had received or simply could not figure out how to deal with a possible foreign intrusion and therefore ignored the advance warnings. After Perry left, *bakufu* officials had no recourse but to address the issue. For the first time in Tokugawa history, the *bakufu* leaders asked for advice from all of the *daimyô*, not just from those who were Tokugawa supporters. Furthermore, the *bakufu* turned to the court for the emperor's opinion on what Japan should do, an unheard-of solicitation. This earthshaking attempt at consultation was necessary not only due to the complexity of the situation, but also because of a *bakufu* leadership shake-up. The reigning *shogun*, taken ill just after Perry arrived, perhaps due to the shock of the American's forceful entry, died shortly after Perry left, and his replacement was simpleminded and immature. At the same time there was tension between several of the most powerful *daimyô* and the *bakufu* senior officials, as well as between particular Tokugawa leaders and the court. Tension among leaders at all levels in Japan was high.

At the *bakufu*'s monthly meeting of August 1854, members of the senior council, composed of those *daimyô* currently in residence in Edo, were polled about what Japan's response should be when the Americans returned. Their answers were based on little, if any, understanding of the issue, and no consensus was forthcoming. Many *daimyô* felt that laws prohibiting the *han* from building modern military defenses should be rescinded, and they should move quickly to build naval ships and refortify and arm the coastal and harbor ramparts. Others believed that Japan should simply open its borders to international commerce. Some thought seclusion should be maintained at all costs, even war. And others simply had no idea how to respond. On the other hand, the firm response from the court in Kyoto was adamant opposition to opening up Japan and a determination to hold off further foreign intrusion at any cost. In fact, whether the officials spoke for "repelling the barbarians," attempting to stall for time, or even accepting some foreign trade, they responded without understanding the seriousness of this threat to an already weakened Tokugawa regime. Nor did they fathom the extent of the advantage modern technology and science gave the Westerners. Only the few students of Dutch studies might have been able to grasp the dramatically inferior position in which the Japanese found themselves.

To further compound the *bakufu*'s problems, on August 21, four Russian ships put in at Nagasaki, and the leader of this expedition demanded that the Japanese settle its northern boundaries with Russia and open one or two ports for trade. The Russians had been pressing against Japan's northern frontiers since the previous century and this time were not to be denied. The issue was Sakhalin just north of **Ezo** (present-day Hokkaido), where Russians raided native villages on a regular basis. Undoubtedly the admiral, Putiatin, would have persisted had not rumors of war between Russia and the Ottoman Empire in the vicinity of the Black Sea made him suddenly withdraw his squadron. In fact war did break out in October 1853. By March 1854, French and British troops had joined with Turkey against Russia in this remote and devastating conflict, known to history as the Crimean War. From the *bakufu*'s perspective this fortuitous clash removed the Russian threat for a while and kept the French and British out of the Japanese picture briefly; however, the Americans were not to be denied. Seeing both an immediate opportunity and a future threat from other imperial powers once the "Eastern Question" was solved, Perry moved forward his return to Edo from the promised one year to February 1854. The *bakufu* would be forced to respond sooner than anticipated.

An American Consulate Is Established

Before Perry's return, the *bakufu*'s senior council did repeal the law which prevented the *han* from building warships and had begun military modernization and arms production at Edo. It would, however, be years before Japan's defenses were substantially improved. Even the efforts by powerful *daimyô*, such as

Shimizu of Satsuma–*han* in the south of Kyushu, to build up their own coastal defenses were meager compared with what was needed. Consequently, when Commodore Perry sailed into the Uraga Channel with six ships and continued to make his way into Edo Bay, it was apparent to *bakufu* officials that negotiations would have to take place. The only questions the Japanese continued to debate were where these discussions would take place and how much the Japanese officials would have to concede to the Americans. It took the negotiators on both sides from the arrival of the first ships on February 13 until March 8 to complete the arrangements. By then nine vessels had entered Edo Bay, and the fleet was within just a few miles of the capital.

The site of the negotiations was a specially constructed building in present-day Yokohama. Thus, after weeks of negotiations over just the location of the discussions, the Japanese succeeded in their primary goal, to keep Perry out of the capital at Edo. The Treaty of Kanagawa was signed on the last day of March in 1854. The language proclaimed "sincere friendship between the two nations" and declared that there "shall be a perfect, permanent, and universal peace" between the United States and the Japanese empire. The heart of the treaty provided for ports at Shimoda at the tip of the Izu Peninsula and Hakodate on the island of Ezo (Hokkaido), to provide the Americans with supplies, especially coal, wood, and water; humane treatment and then return of shipwrecked sailors; free movement within a range of about a twenty-mile radius for American inhabitants of the port cities rather than confinement like that of the Dutch in Nagasaki; automatic conferral of any privileges the Japanese might grant in the future to any other foreign power; and the right of the U.S. to assign a consul to reside in Shimoda to look after American interests. Although commercial exchange was not included in this treaty, it was foreshadowed. Japan's seclusion was ended. Within a short time the Russians, French, and British would all negotiate similar treaties with the *bakufu*. And within fourteen more years, the *bakufu* itself would no longer exist.

In 1855, Townsend Harris, a hard-drinking, single, unsuccessful businessman applied for the job of American Consul in

Japan. In spite of his poor record, Harris, then in China, was granted the position. He sailed for Japan immediately, arriving at Shimoda in August 1856. Surprisingly, over the next two years Harris managed to find a place to live, engage a Dutch translator, and gain the respect of the Japanese around him. Finally, by November 1857, Harris secured a meeting in Edo with Hotta Masayoshi, the senior member of the *bakufu* council, who, happily for Harris, was the one high official who accepted the inevitability of foreign trade. The American was aided in his discussions by the fear which the resumed British and French military operations in China had engendered in Japan's capital. Harris's negotiations resulted in the July 1858 "Treaty of Amity and Commerce Between the United States and Japan," a treaty highly favorable to the United States and clearly opposed by many of Japan's *daimyô* and by the imperial court at Kyoto. The most significant features of this treaty were the adding of three additional ports and towns to be opened to Americans over the next four years; opening up of Edo and then Osaka four and five years hence for American residence and trade; setting of commercial tariffs; prosecuting American criminals in American courts (**extraterritoriality**); allowing the purchase and/or construction of American-designed ships of all sorts including war vessels; and, finally, setting up a Japanese consulate in Washington, D.C. Around the same time the Dutch, Russians, and British signed similar treaties with the Japanese *bakufu*, and all of the foreigners, including the Americans, soon gained "**most-favored nation**" status, guaranteeing that each foreign nation would receive the same benefits and privileges extended to any of the others.

Fukuzawa Sails to America

Shortly after the Townsend Harris treaty became effective, Fukuzawa Yûkichi arrived in Edo to take over his domain's school of Dutch studies. The changed circumstances caused by the powerful American presence became immediately evident to Fukuzawa when he visited the treaty port of Yokohama. He could see that it would be more advantageous to emphasize English over Dutch. During the next several months Fukuzawa

Fukuzawa (seated, far right) and fellow crew members about to leave on the *Kanrinmaru* for America, 1860. (Used with permission of the Fukuzawa Memorial Center at Keiô University.)

focused on both his new language studies and on schemes to travel to America. In this latter project he was aided by the positive historical role his domain had played under the rule of the Tokugawa *bakufu* and by his personal associations in high places.

Nakatsu-*han*, though fairly low in the domain hierarchy, had been a part of the *bakufu*'s inner circle from the beginning of the Tokugawa Era. At this critical moment in the late 1850s Fukuzawa sought ways to take advantage of his *han*'s positive relationship with the *bakufu* and, by extension, with Japan's new relationship with the United States. By 1860 Fukuzawa's manipulation of personal associations and his utilitarian educational achievements secured for him a place in the new international exchange between America and Japan. Fukuzawa began yet another personal adventure.

One of the provisions of the **Harris Treaty** was that the Japanese must send a delegation to Washington, D.C., to exchange official signed memoranda of understanding on the treaty's specific stipulations. A second provision stated that Japan could build or purchase new ships through the good offices of the United States. In fulfillment of both these two provisions, the *bakufu* decided to buy a sailing vessel from the Dutch, outfit it, learn to operate it, and sail it across the Pacific Ocean as a companion to the American steamship that would carry the official Washington-bound Japanese delegation. Fukuzawa, not the least bit intimidated by the fact that his countrymen had never sailed a vessel beyond the shores of Japan's borders, was determined to be a part of this expedition.

He used his newly claimed knowledge of English, slight though it might yet be; his association with those close to *bakufu* officials; and, perhaps most importantly, the personal introduction through a friend to the ship's commodore to secure himself a place on the sailing vessel. Successful in his entreaties, he joined the crew of the *Kanrinmaru* as Commodore Kimura's personal steward. He was one of ninety-six crew members, including doctors, engineers, stokers, and sailors, who made this pioneering voyage. Only one of the Japanese aboard ship had any previous experience sailing on the open seas. This was the returned castaway Nakamura Manjirô who, having lived and gone to school in America for several years, proved to be a much better interpreter than Fukuzawa.

With very few exceptions, no one among the two shiploads of Japanese to America achieved much understanding of that distant country, its culture, or its politics. In fact, for the most part, the party of Japanese officials who landed in San Francisco and then went overland to Washington, D.C., and Fukuzawa's associates on the *Kanrinmaru* who sailed only to San Francisco found the whole event more discomforting and troublesome than adventurous. Most would have preferred to stay in Japan. By contrast, Fukuzawa expressed great enthusiasm for the trip. In his autobiography he retrospectively proclaimed with both amazement and great satisfaction that the voyage confirmed the scientific and technological progress Japan had achieved in such a short time. He wrote that it had been only "about seven years after the first sight of a steamship,

[and] after only about five years of practice, [that] the Japanese people made a trans-Pacific crossing without help from foreign experts. I think," he concluded, "we can without undue pride boast before the world of this courage and skill." Evaluation of this self-applause must compare Fukuzawa's statements with those written by the seasoned American captain and sailors who accompanied this expedition. The American captain, John Brooke, described the Japanese officers and crew as ignorant and unable to manage the ship under full sail. Consequently, shortly after the *Kanrinmaru* left Japan on February 10, 1860, it was the Americans who guided and manned the ship. Perhaps by the time Fukuzawa wrote his autobiography in 1899 his memory had dimmed in proportion to the growth of his feelings of nationalism and thus he could assign full credit for expert sailing to his compatriots. The voyage to San Francisco must have been a much more harrowing journey than Fukuzawa recalled, for the entire time the crew was in San Francisco, the *Kanrinmaru* was in drydock undergoing significant repairs. She received two new masts, new sails, and repairs to the propeller and copper fittings. It is a wonder that the ship, whoever was in control, completed the transpacific voyage. On the other hand, Fukuzawa could be truly proud of the return trip, as the Japanese crew sailed back to Japan without American help.

This might not have been the mission Fukuzawa anticipated but, thanks to his scientific study at Ogata's school, he benefitted from his almost two-month stay in San Francisco more than most of his associates. Even though he had never seen electric lights or a telegraph system or an operating sugar refinery before, he could follow the detailed explanation provided, for he understood the engineering principles involved. These technological feats, however, did not surprise him as much as the waste evident in America. "First of all, there seemed to be an enormous waste of iron everywhere. In garbage piles, on the seashores—everywhere—I found lying old oil tins, empty cans, and broken tools." Such extravagant waste was "remarkable" to all of the Japanese, who were so careful at home to reclaim even the smallest nail after a fire. In the end, though, it was the picture of scientific knowledge and technological application that he carried back with him. For this short "mission to America," as Fukuzawa called it, intensified his obsession with Western science, technology, and culture and initiated what was to become a lifetime desire to disseminate Western learning to the people of Japan.

Fukuzawa was not surprised that the first news he was told upon returning from America in June 1860 was that the *shogun*'s regent had been assassinated. Ii Naosuke was an unbending autocrat and appeared to be a supporter of the foreigners. There had been fierce opposition to the treaties with America and the other Western powers, which had manifested itself in 1858 with a change of leadership in the *bakufu* council just before the signing of the Harris Treaty. Hotta, who had negotiated the treaty, was superseded in July 1858 by the appointment of Ii Naosuke as regent for the new twelve-year-old *shogun* whom Ii had favored in a fight over the *shogunal* line of succession. Although his appointment as regent reflected anti-treaty sentiments, in recognition of the reality of Western superiority throughout the Far East, Ii signed the treaty in August without soliciting further advice from powerful *daimyô* or other *bakufu* officials. Though anti-foreign in principle, Ii was pragmatic and felt Japan needed to rebuild its military and grow economically before attempting to throw out the barbarian, and thus he gave the appearance of favoring the treaties. This practical policy proved too accommodating for many *samurai* both within the *bakufu* and among the more powerful anti-Tokugawa domains. Over the next few years anti-foreignism, which ranged from rudeness to murder, was the rule. A number of nameless foreign sailors, a few foreign officials, and Japanese who appeared sympathetic to these outsiders were murdered. In fact, a bit later, in January 1861, Townsend Harris's secretary would be killed. The movement to "expel the barbarians" was popular and gaining in favor. All those who even grudgingly accepted the treaty provisions risked life and limb.

And so, Fukuzawa took the news of Ii's assassination in stride. It wasn't that he didn't recognize that the same anti-foreign feeling that propelled the assassin's blade toward officials in high office might also be extended to those who, like himself, were simply involved with Western studies. He tried to be cautious, but he remained determined to continue his own study of English and Western learning and to teach these subjects at his school. He was gratified by the fact that the number of pupils interested in foreign studies grew in spite of a climate of terror. There was no turning back for Fukuzawa or for his country. Even the *bakufu*, torn apart as it was by growing opposition to Tokugawa rule, recognized that foreigners were in Japan to stay, at least for the time being, and hired Fukuzawa as a "translator of messages from foreign legations." In this capacity he translated into Japanese the Dutch renderings of English documents. For his own study, however, he practiced first with the English versions in an attempt to perfect his facility with the language he had predicted would be the more important.

A Mission to Europe

Fukuzawa's position as a translator for the *bakufu* not only brought him a steady salary in addition to his *samurai* stipend but gave him access to information about foreign relations. Therefore, when the government decided to send a delegation to Europe to renegotiate the 1858 treaties with France and Britain, Fukuzawa was eager to join. The primary purpose of the diplomatic mission was to try to get the foreign powers to put off the opening of two additional ports and the cities of Edo and Osaka for foreign commerce and residency. Such an increase in foreign presence, the *bakufu* believed, would intensify anti-foreign activities, which were already consuming the *bakufu*'s attention and weakening its control over the domains. Takenouchi Yasunori, Foreign Affairs Commissioner, was chosen to lead the mission. In the spring of 1861, he sought the advice of Dr. Philipp Franz von Siebold, a German who had resided and taught in Nagasaki during the twenties. Siebold suggested that the Japanese add Holland, Prussia, Russia, and Portugal to the itinerary to provide the visitors with a more comprehensive picture of Europe and broaden the scope of the mission to include scientific and cultural observation as well as diplomatic discussions. By November 1861, the participants were chosen, a steamship was offered by the British, and the British and French agreed to pay for the round trip. Fukuzawa had not been named to the translator position he sought, although two of his friends in his office had been summoned to serve. Fukuzawa was frantic not to be left out of this new foreign adventure. Finally, just before the ship was to sail, Fukuzawa received notice that he had been ordered to join the translator cohort. The whole group, numbering about forty, steamed out of Edo on January 21, 1862.

The voyage was a long one: from China to Singapore, through the Indian Ocean to the Red Sea, across the Suez by train to Cairo, where another ship took the Japanese to Marseille, France, and, finally, on to Paris by train on April 7. Once in Paris, the mission was stalemated by their uncooperative French counterparts, and it was decided to leave the difficult diplomatic resolutions for the British meetings. Meanwhile the group had two weeks for sightseeing. Fukuzawa indicated in his autobiography the sort of information he found to be important. "For instance, when I saw a hospital, I wanted to know how it was run—who paid the running expenses; when I visited a bank, I wished to learn how the money was deposited and paid out." By a process of questions and observations, then, he "learned something about the postal system and the military conscription then in force in France but not in England." He commented that "a perplexing institution was representative government." He asked about election laws and how parliaments worked. Fukuzawa was acquiring information that would be set forth in his books about the West and knowledge that would be of use in the 1870s when Japan redesigned its political and economic institutions.

In London the group's visit happened to coincide with the Fourth International Exposition held in South Kensington. The Japanese were encouraged to attend. Quoting from Fukuzawa's diary of the trip, W.G. Beasley (1995) illustrates further Fukuzawa's keen eye and his strong interest in observing things Western. "Manufactures from all countries and newly-developed machines have been collected here. . . . Steam machines to make cloth from cotton and wool, chemicals to make ice in the summer, steam-powered equipment for pumping water, all are here. There is fire-fighting apparatus, ingenious clocks, agricultural tools, horse trappings, kitchens, ship models, old books, and paintings without number." The Japanese must have created quite an exotic spectacle, for a group photograph of the highest-level officials, taken at the Exposition, showed them dressed formally from head to toe. Perched on top of their shaved heads sat small, stiff triangular hats (*eboshi*); their bodies were covered with long overjackets (*haori*) over wide pants (*hakama*), and on their feet they wore split-toed socks (*tabi*), which were slid into sandals (*zori*) held on by one thong between the big toe and the second toe. Each man wore his long and short sword to show he was of the elite *samurai* class.

Fukuzawa's study of the West continued as the mission moved on to Holland, where all of the Japanese felt most comfortable because of the Dutch language. From there the group traveled to Prussia. In Berlin Fukuzawa observed a debate in Parliament in spite of the fact he knew no German. A few lower ranking members of the mission, including Fukuzawa, had a photo taken in Berlin. This pictured a more relaxed group than the one in London, but still in formal *samurai* attire, just not displaying the more formal jackets, pants, and braided coat closings of the class of officials. For this shot one member of the group wore a wide-brimmed sedge hat, and the others were bareheaded, showing the shaved *samurai* haircut. All, of course, had swords. The next stop was St. Petersburg, the capital of Russia, where diplomatic discussions deadlocked on the northern border issues concerning the island of Sakhalin. Fukuzawa stood for formal photographs taken in Berlin and St. Petersburg which show him in formal attire but hatless. His pose showed off his family crests and swords. He, too, was a *samurai*, if one of lower rank. The foreigners could not distinguish the subtle differences of status indicated by the attire that so thoroughly annoyed Fukuzawa during his years growing up in Nakatsu. In the several European cities visited, Fukuzawa took notes on hospitals, museums, factories, libraries, schools, and so forth. He was in Europe to study Western manners and culture, not to critique ancient Japanese customs. The mission ended its European tour in Lisbon.

Fukuzawa and the rest of the entourage then sailed for home in late October, arriving in Edo January 29, 1863, having been away for a little more than one year.

Fukuzawa remarked in his autobiography that he returned from Europe to an even more violently anti-foreign Japan than he had left. On the other hand, his school for Western studies was continuing to grow, and his work for the government had become even more essential. The sensitivity of his position with the Tokugawa *bakufu* revealed itself in documents he had to translate, which dealt with murder and mayhem against foreign nationals. In fact, Fukuzawa became quite worried about his own safety given his known foreign interests and work as a translator. He lived in the midst of a country confronted by economic demands from the West, peasant uprisings in the countryside, and unrest and insurgency in the cities and towns. Dissatisfaction with the *bakufu*'s handling of both foreign and domestic controversies finally led to revolutionary actions by the strongest Western domains. It was obvious that foreigners were not going to go away, and it was equally obvious, at least to some, that the Tokugawa *bakufu* would not be able to stave off its own demise much longer. Fukuzawa would soon find himself quite literally in the crossfire when the military units clashed in Edo. The question that he would have to answer was whether he would take a side in the battles to come and if so, whether it would be with the *bakufu* or with the imperialist rebels.

Fukuzawa Sidesteps the Civil War

Fukuzawa had learned much from his trips to America and Europe. One of the clearest impressions he gained was that his country lagged far behind the West in scientific and technological progress. He might have bragged that his knowledge from Dutch studies made it possible for him to understand many facets of the West, but, at the same time, he recognized the long distance Japan must travel to pull even with the foreigners. He did not, however, predict the actual downfall of the backward looking Tokugawa government. Consequently, he tried to keep a low profile while translating for the *bakufu* and running his school of Western studies. He continued to fear personal harm from anti-foreign sources, but he expected that eventually his compatriots would come to their senses and recognize the importance of foreign learning. When that happened, he expected that an enlightened Tokugawa *bakufu* would take the reigns of government more firmly in hand and make appropriate changes.

However, by the mid-1860s it was clear to some astute officials, both within the *shogun*'s council and in the leadership ranks of the richest and most powerful domains, that Japan was going to have to dramatically change politically, economically, and socially. Attempts were begun within the *shogun*'s council, including among those whose appointments had been favored by the court, to implement reforms that might appeal to strongly anti-*bakufu* and pro-court *han*. It was hoped that such changes would appease the particularly violent *samurai* who were responsible for most anti-foreigner activities. These *samurai*, known as *shishi*, "men of high purpose," proclaimed as their slogan *sonnô jôi*, "revere the emperor and expel the foreigner." Residing primarily in the coastal *han* of western Japan, in Chôshu (on Honshu), Satsuma and Saga (on Kyushu), and Tosa (on Shikoku), they did everything within their power to cause friction between the *bakufu* officials and the foreigners, while proclaiming their own allegiance to the emperor and his court in Kyoto. In apparent contradiction, the *shishi* also urged their own *han* officials to buy warships and other military equipment from the "hated" foreign powers. In addition, the *daimyô* agreed to send clan members abroad, first illegally and then legally, to study such subjects as naval engineering, chemistry, and medicine from these same hated Western powers. This posture might appear contradictory until one realizes that the rebel leaders in these *han* were primarily concerned with regaining both the land and power they had surrendered to the Tokugawa in the seventeenth century and that anti-foreignism, with its multi-faceted interpretations, seemed the perfect foil for weakening the *bakufu*. Indeed, strengthening *han* knowledge of science and technology would provide the power necessary to destroy the Tokugawa family's central control.

Civil Strife

In the spring of 1863 the *bakufu* finally agreed to imperial demands that Japan "expel" the foreigners and set a date in June at which time the port of Yokohama would be closed. In fact, the *bakufu* had no intention of closing Japan again; the senior counselors knew only too well that they did not have the military power to achieve such an objective. Unfortunately, the Chôshu *daimyô*, assuming this date and cause to be authoritative, fired his *han*'s coastal guns on foreign ships in the Strait of Shimonoseki, causing Americans and French to fire back. Later these foreign warships were joined by those of England and Holland in a military action that essentially destroyed Chôshu's coastal defenses. Such a show of superior military force caused this anti-foreign domain to turn to the West for advice and equipment as its leaders determined to modernize their *han*'s defenses. Shortly afterwards, Satsuma's capital of Kagoshima, at the tip of Kyushu, was fired upon and much of the town destroyed by British warships. This was in support of British demands that Satsuma pay reparations for, and execute the killers of, a British merchant murdered in the fall of 1862. These two powerful *han*, then, learned firsthand of the power of the West and turned it to their advantage as they rebuilt their defenses and modernized their citizen armies. Meanwhile, the *bakufu* officials were stuck with a policy of anti-foreignism that had gone beyond what they had anticipated and with the economic consequences of *han* actions, which in the end harmed the central government more than the domains.

Fukuzawa Yûkichi was closer to these events than he would have liked. When he returned from Europe in January 1863, he settled back into his translation job with the *bakufu*. Although he was only obliged to go to the office a few times a month, the work he did there was crucial to explicating Japan's foreign policy. It was, for example, Fukuzawa who was called upon to translate the sensitive documents that contained the demands of the British in the case of the murdered British merchant. Therefore, he was, at least indirectly, involved with the negotiations between the *bakufu* and the British chargé d'affaires over the demanded indemnity, apology, and punishment of the criminals. Fukuzawa worried constantly about his own safety as he watched anti-foreignism grow at home, while, at the same time, the foreign powers made clear in the diplomatic statements he translated that they had no intention of leaving Japan.

By both his *bakufu* job and his *samurai* status within the Nakatsu clan, Fukuzawa owed allegiance to the *bakufu*. In 1864, this relationship was further enhanced when he was made a **hatamoto**, a vassal of the *bakufu* itself, with an additional stipend of one hundred and fifty *koku* of rice, a realized additional wealth of about one hundred *koku*. At the same time, by his interest in foreign books and foreign culture, he continued to call attention to himself as a supporter of the West. Fukuzawa was aware of the tenuous position these associations placed him in. As tension grew within the *baku-han* system and bullets flew between the foreigners and the clans in western Japan, he tried to protect himself and his family by remaining in the background as much as possible. He moderated his speech and tried not to discuss matters of social or political significance with people he was not sure he could fully trust. He even set forward evacuation plans in the event that his house might become a battleground. Not completely silenced, however, he did speak out against his students joining the *bakufu* forces when an army was being raised to punish Chôshu. This was not the result of favoring the powerful Chôshu domain, but rather of concern for the lives and welfare of his students. Fukuzawa remained, in fact, a *bakufu* supporter, if a tentative and frightened one.

By 1866, the *bakufu* had dug itself into even deeper debt to the foreign legations. It had agreed to pay both its own assigned indemnity and that of Satsuma for the Englishman's murder; it had agreed to open the additional treaty ports; and it had made commercial concessions to the various foreign powers. Meanwhile, the *bakufu*'s strength in contrast with the western *han* was weakened by heavier financial burdens, increasing obligations to the imperial court in Kyoto, and by abolition of *sankin-kôtai*, law of alternate attendance. In fact, this last change meant that each domain, which no longer had to send its *daimyô* and his entourage to Edo in alternate years or maintain property there, accumulated great savings, which could be put toward *han* defense. As the scholar Marius Jansen concludes, by this time the *bakufu* had become just one of the regional powers. This weakened *bakufu* would find it impossible to withstand the pressures of the other regional powers, such as Chôshu, Satsuma, and Tosa.

In 1866, a *shishi* leader of Tosa, Sakamoto Ryôma, brought together Saigô Takamori of Satsuma and Kido Kôin of Chôshu; and all three agreed to an alliance against the *bakufu*. Later that year this was put to the test as the *bakufu* sent an expeditionary force all the way to Chôshu to chastise the recalcitrant *han* and bring it back into the *bakufu*'s fold. Edo had hoped to gain support from the other domains in its fight against Chôshu, but the agreement among the powerful western *han* precluded any of them joining with the *bakufu*. The expedition ended in the defeat and withdrawal of *bakufu* troops. The demise of Tokugawa power was drawing near.

Fukuzawa, of course, in his roles as *hatamoto* and government translator was well informed about the mission against Chôshu. The Fukuzawa scholar Norio Tamaki has translated a crucial petition from Fukuzawa to the government about the Chôshu situation. According to this document, Fukuzawa saw immediately that the *bakufu* would have difficulty defeating Chôshu, which had "hoarded munitions secretly for two years, thoroughly transformed their weaponry and strategy into the western style and united their people to face up to the government forces." Fukuzawa followed this analysis with the following advice: "At the moment I beg for your forgiveness to say that the *bakufu* would not be able to win instantly, and I am deeply worried about it. Therefore I would like to propose that the *bakufu* should consider employing foreign troops to crush Chôshu at a stroke." Recognizing the expense involved in such a plan, Fukuzawa proposed to pay for the foreign intervention with a combination of income seized from the defeated *han* and the issuance of twenty-year bonds. Of course, this suggestion was not acted upon by the *bakufu*, but it does reflect two important characteristics of Fukuzawa: It shows his continued loyalty to the central authority, and it reveals his understanding of basic banking and finance principles he had observed in the West.

The *bakufu*'s futile campaign against Chôshu was one further indication that the *baku-han* system was nearing its end. More and more the real decisions were being made in Kyoto with the support of the imperial loyalists from the powerful domains. In February 1867, the reigning emperor died at thirty-five from smallpox. His successor, his fifteen-year-old son, Mutsuhito, soon to be known as the Emperor Meiji, ascended to the throne. At this moment those determined to destroy the *bakufu* elevated the cry of "revere the emperor" to new heights as they demanded the resignation of the *shogun* and the acceptance of the new emperor as the only ruler of all of Japan. Kidô of Chôshu and Saigô of Satsuma signed an agreement of alliance and put their troops at the disposal of the emperor. At first they simply pressured the *shogun* to withdraw from Kyoto. When that proved ineffective, toward the end of that year they demanded that he resign.

Fukuzawa's Final Service to the Bakufu

During that last year, when the *bakufu* was still ostensibly in charge of Japan, Japan sent yet another mission to America. The practical purpose of this small mission was to take possession of a warship that had been commissioned and paid for in 1863. In fact, two ships had been bought at this time but only one delivered due to America's Civil War. Finally, in 1866, it was deemed necessary to go in person to Washington, D.C., to claim the ship and, at the same time, to purchase weapons. At this point the *bakufu* still believed that it could subdue the rebellious domains and that additional ships and guns would be useful in this endeavor. When Fukuzawa heard about the mission, he pressed its leader, an assistant minister of the treasury and naval engineer, to take him along. After several entreaties, Fukuzawa was included in the party of nine, which set off in February 1867 aboard one of the new fast steamers the United States had launched to provide a packet service between Japan and America.

Fukuzawa was designated the mission's financial officer. In this capacity he dealt with the U. S. banking system through the use of letters of credit and learned firsthand about the effects of inflation on paper money. Fortunately, he had chosen to exchange *bakufu* currency for bills of exchange backed by Mexican dollars before he left Japan. When he exchanged these for cash in New York and Washington, he understood more clearly the significance of his decision. As Professor Tamaki concludes, "The most important direct outcome of this mission for Fukuzawa was his ever firmer knowledge of Western business practices." In the shorter term Fukuzawa's business acumen saved the *bakufu* considerable money, which could have been lost through unfavorable exchange rates and inflation. Unfortunately the *bakufu* had little enough time left to make use of either the military purchases or the money saved.

When Fukuzawa returned to Edo in July 1867, he discovered the central government in great flux and the western domains gaining influence with the young Emperor Meiji and his advisors in Kyoto. During the summer Sakamoto Ryôma of Tosa circulated an eight-point program that amounted to *de facto* recognition of the primary position of the emperor and the **restoration** of imperial supremacy of power. Included among the points Sakamoto made were return to imperial rule; establishment of a two-house legislature; counselors drawn from court nobles and *daimyô*; openly arrived-at foreign agreements; and the establishment of a new legal code. The *shogun*'s resignation was demanded in late fall 1867. The Tokugawa *bakufu* was being pushed out of power.

Two significant events coincided in the beginning of 1868. First, the Emperor Meiji abolished the office of *shogun* and proclaimed his own power as supreme. Secondly, the *han* forces, believing that the *bakufu* was not going to depart quietly, chased the *shogun* and his army back to Edo from Kyoto. The coalition of Western-style *han* soldiers under Saigô's command fought the *shogun*'s army as it fled from Kyoto and then in the streets of Edo. In the spring the inevitable surrender of the *shogun*'s army meant the war was essentially over. The loyal supporters of the Emperor had proved militarily superior. It would be another year, however, before all pro-*bakufu* forces were subdued. Led by a *bakufu* loyalist, a small military unit fled north, making its final stand at the treaty port of Hakodate in Ezo (Hokkaido), finally to be defeated by imperial forces in a bloody last battle during the spring of 1869.

Fukuzawa: "A Non-Partisan"

Fukuzawa, a member of the pro-*bakufu* Nakatsu *han*, one of the *shogun*'s *hatamoto,* and a low-level Tokugawa bureaucrat, did not openly oppose his superiors, who were trying to hold on to power. In fact, he found reasons to find fault with both sides in this *baku-han* civil war. In his 1899 autobiography he called himself a "non-partisan in the restoration." In political conversations with colleagues as the 1867 mission returned from America, Fukuzawa ventured the following opinion on the outlook for the *shogun*: "The *shogun*ate cannot hold the country together much longer. It seems to me that all the clans might get together and form a federation like Germany." With the clarity of hindsight, he summed up his view of the crisis in government in the manner of a rational bystander. He called the *shogun*'s government "bureaucratic, oppressive, conservative, anti-foreign" and therefore did not like it and would not side with it. On the other hand, those who followed the "imperial cause" were worse because they were "still more anti-foreign and violent in their action." Fukuzawa, who claimed that he was not politically ambitious, was determined not to cast his lot with either side. He then went on to speak of the "pompous arrogance" of the Tokugawa men and began a tirade against the feudal status system, which had plagued him from early childhood. Finally, he concluded, after three trips abroad and extensive study of Western thought and culture, that he simply could not countenance the anti-foreign stance either side displayed, and he did not care to join in either side's ignorance.

Even when the fighting reached Edo, Fukuzawa refused to be drawn in. He condemned the **Sat-Chô** imperialist army for "they were actually murdering people, setting houses on fire, and declaring that even if the whole land were to be reduced to ashes, Japan must be kept from foreign influence." He noted that the masses echoed this anti-foreign cry, as they rioted in great confusion and destruction throughout Edo and the rest of the country. Just the same, he would not follow the advice of some of his associates and fight for the *shogun*'s cause. As he told a friend, if the fighting came near his house he would have to run away to save his life. When he was told where retainers of the *shogun* should gather to make a last stand, he replied to his informant that he should count Fukuzawa's household out.

The fighting came within five miles of his house, but his family was not disturbed. Astonishingly, at the very time that Edo was in chaos and fires could be seen all around, Fukuzawa was completing a transaction for a large piece of land and the vacated mansion of a *daimyô*. He had plans to build his family a new house and his students a new school. While everyone else was "making bundles of belongings ready for escape to the country," he hired idle workmen to build his new house and a student dormitory. The "soldiers of Chôshu" did come, and they commandeered his new building for their quarters, but he

Fukuzawa and his two eldest sons L. Sutejirô and R. Ichitarô, mid-1870s.(Used with permission of the Fukuzawa Memorial Center at Keiô University.)

found them disciplined and peaceful. No members of his family or students at the school were harmed or threatened by these soldiers. Some of his students supported and joined the *bakufu*, while others ran off to fight for the imperial cause. And yet there was no conflict on the school's grounds. Strangely, this chaotic time proved auspicious for Fukuzawa. Defeat of the *shogun*'s forces, establishment of the emperor's authority, and the completion of Fukuzawa's new school were all achieved simultaneously. If Japan were now to enter a period of peace and stability, Fukuzawa believed he would thrive.

A Family Man

In 1861, between his two trips abroad in the early 1860s, Fukuzawa married Toki Okin, also of the Nakatsu clan. She was the daughter of a *samurai*, as would be expected, but, in defiance of Tokugawa social laws, she belonged to an upper-level *samurai* family. It will be remembered that the dividing line between upper- and lower-class *samurai* was sacrosanct, never to be crossed. Although, as Fukuzawa described in detail, there were hundreds of distinctions between individual *samurai* families, everyone was grouped into either the upper or lower ranks, and the division between these ranks could not be breached. The fact that Fukuzawa married into the upper rank reflected both the continued weakening of the Tokugawa social laws and Fukuzawa's own abhorrence of the demeaning implications of such a feudal classification. At the time of their marriage Yūkichi was twenty-eight, had worked in the capital for a couple of years, and had sailed to America and back. Okin, his new bride, just seventeen, was also living in Edo, where her father served the Nakatsu *daimyō* as a high-level minister.

Before his marriage Fukuzawa had lived on the Nakatsu-*han* estate in Edo. Afterward, he and Okin moved briefly to a house in a different part of town but soon returned to the Nakatsu estate. It was here that their first two sons were born, Ichitarō in 1863, and Sutejirō in 1865. Each time Fukuzawa moved, he needed to consider both the needs of his family and those of his school, which grew in number of students and educational breadth. In the spring of 1868, amid the turmoil of the *baku-han* fighting in Edo, the family and school moved to Hamamatsu-cho, the area where Yūkichi and Okin had begun their married life. That April, the new house and buildings were completed, and the civil war had ended. One month later, in May, Okin gave birth to their third child, a daughter, named San and later called Sato. In 1870, a second daughter, Fusa, was born. After that, there were three more daughters, followed by two sons, nine children in all over a twenty-year span. Through all of these births Okin maintained good health. Yūkichi, however, noted that after the sixth child "we hired wet nurses because we were afraid the mother's health might be impaired." Another reason for adding to the household might simply have been the increased wealth of the family. By the time the sixth child was born in 1876, Yūkichi, who was always very careful with his finances, could easily afford the eight or so servants in the household, including wet nurses.

Although Yûkichi did not elaborate publicly on the nature of his relationship with his wife, the marriage obviously satisfied him. He spoke of the love and harmony that pervaded his household and implied a high level of comfort with his wife, Okin. Also, he proudly stated in several publications that he did not have any wish to participate in the usual womanizing that was prevalent among his social class during the **Meiji Period**, nor did he ever take a concubine, as many high-ranking bureaucrats in the new Meiji government had. He saw no point in initiating a visit to a *geisha* house, but, on the other hand, he was "not put out by the gaiety" should he find himself in circumstances where *geisha* were included. There is every indication from his own reminiscences and from his formal writings on women that he was a firm promoter of monogamous marital relationships.

More than likely it was Yûkichi who took the lead in deciding the role these two parents would play in the upbringing of their many children. On the other, hand his ideas on raising children were so liberal, and the results so apparently successful and yet so temperate and restrained, that it would seem likely that Okin approved of his methods. Yûkichi used the term "parents" when he spoke of nurturing his children and thus appeared to give Okin credit as well. In describing the children, he emphasized that "we make no distinction at all in affection and position between boys and girls. . . . I should not have regretted having nine daughters." And again, "my children are all equal." Fukuzawa undoubtedly believed that this was so, though, as we shall see, the girls were not treated the same as the boys when it came to higher education and approved adult roles. Just the same, for his status and the era his children grew up in, he was unusually evenhanded with his sons and daughters.

Fukuzawa's method of child rearing was quite liberal for any time period. He stated that he and his wife were more concerned with their children's food than their clothes, undoubtedly reflecting their father's notorious disregard for his own appearance. Emphasis was placed on physical fitness, and so the children were allowed much latitude in robust play. As a result, "we had to be content to see a few things broken once in a while. We were not going to scold them for making tears in the paper doors and a few nicks in the furniture." The extent of his discipline was to give them "a serious look" when it was time to stop. In this household, he wrote, "there is not the usual distinction between strict father and loving mother. In strictness we are both strict; in love we are both loving. We, parents and children, live together like trusting friends."

Perhaps the most astonishing attitudes toward parental authority exercised in the household were those related to education. It might be expected that Fukuzawa would be a strict teacher, demanding early and sustained attention to study. Not so. He believed the children should spend their first four or five years simply playing and growing. Over the next three years he would show them a few examples of the reading and writing of *kanji* (pictographs) they would eventually have to learn, but even then there would not be reading lessons. The children were "left perfectly free to romp about." It was not until they reached nine or ten that he began to give them regular lessons, and even then, he taught them only during specified hours with careful attention not to injure their health. In this Fukuzawa was, to some extent, copying his own educational history, which had been considered lax at that time. He was even older than his children when he began serious study, and yet, by the time he was nineteen he had studied Chinese and Japanese subjects and begun Dutch. Furthermore, in contrast with most households, the Fukuzawa parents did not praise their children for reading books, even particularly complex ones. Rather, they were praised for being lively and physically adventurous.

The household was an active one and continuously increasing in size. In 1870, he brought his beloved mother and his niece, his brother's only child, from Nakatsu to live with the family. Later Okin's mother also joined the household. In the 1870s the household included a total of sixteen children and adults; and the family had not, at that time, increased to its largest number. Fortunately, Fukuzawa's income increased steadily, too, and the house and the adjoining school, which

Fukuzawa began building in 1868, were completely paid for. Because he had a lifelong aversion to debt, he paid the agreed-upon price for this *daimyô* owned estate before he began his new construction. In fact, he delivered the money while *bakufu* and *han* troops were fighting in Edo. The mere fact that as a *samurai* he could participate in this financial transaction, and that the *daimyô* was permitted to sell him the land set aside for domain purposes, illustrated the Tokugawa *bakufu*'s powerlessness to regulate *samurai* activities.

Before 1868 Fukuzawa still received his *samurai* stipend from the Nakatsu *han* and his *bakufu* stipend as a *hatamoto*. He also had a salary for his work as a translator. In addition to this, he began to earn money for translation work done on a private basis, for which he charged high rates. But his largest source of money was royalties from his writing. He began publishing a Japanese/English dictionary, copied from a Chinese/English dictionary, as early as 1860. After his second trip abroad in 1862, he wrote the first volume of a three-volume work entitled *Conditions in the West*, which was published in 1867. This signaled the beginning of a successful career in writing and publishing, for it earned him substantial royalties through sales of more than 150,000 copies. Volume I included descriptions of institutions, particularly schools, libraries, and museums; the organization of governments, companies, and armies and navies; operations and functions of newspapers and financial institutions; and national histories of America, Holland, and England. It is clear from the number of copies sold and the many more sold in pirated editions that the small reading public was eager to learn more about the West. The year 1867 might have been characterized as anti-foreign in *bakufu* and *han* official circles, but the educated public was interested in learning more about this "enemy." The second volume, which was a freely translated and augmented version of a high school text on political economy, was published in 1870. Fukuzawa's literary success proved to be an economic windfall that made it possible to pay for the land for his new house and school outright and provide for such a large household.

A New Concept in Education

Keiô Gijuku, or *Keiô* Private School, was named after the era that ended with the restoration of the emperor in 1868. The concept for the *gijuku* came from Fukuzawa's description of schools in England, which he had just finished writing about in *Conditions in the West*. The school itself was patterned after an English public school (called private in America), and its curriculum was based primarily on English language texts, particularly the many books that Fukuzawa had brought back from his three trips abroad. The organization of the school simulated a corporate body in the sense that teachers and students were to be equal, and everyone was to contribute to the administration and upkeep of the school and its buildings as well as the teaching and studying. In this ideal circumstance, no tuition was paid but contributions were made in labor and money. This system was short-lived, for beginning in 1869 the smaller domains were absorbed by the government, and by 1871, all *han* were abolished and *samurai* stipends cut dramatically. As a result, students no longer had money that could be easily contributed to the operations of the school, and by the second year of operation tuition had to be charged.

When Fukuzawa opened his new school in April 1868, he proclaimed, "We have gathered together as a corporation to found a school, to collaborate with and cultivate each other in the study of Western learning. . . . We have opened the doors of the school wide to the public to allow all men, regardless of their status as *samurai* or commoner, to come and participate in our program." (In fact, very few commoners, who had no stipends, could attend.) He went on to give a brief history of Western learning in Japan and to declare that this school would be modeled on Western schools. Finally, he spoke of his goals for those who would come from far and wide "to nourish their ability, increase their knowledge, be courteous in their deportment, and faithful in all relations." In other documents he set forward the rules and regulations for classroom activities, dining room decorum, exercise, and cleaning of the buildings. For example: "The members of the Corporation make learning their life work; therefore, under no circumstance shall they draw their swords"; and cleaning of rooms shall include "dusting and sweeping" and opening and closing the doors and windows each day; and "reading books on a dining-room chair occasionally when one is tired of sitting formally at one's desk will be tolerated"; after dinner "all residents shall climb trees, play ball games, or engage in other sports." The class schedule was completely devoted to the works of Western scholars of such subjects as American history, "natural" philosophy, geography, elementary science, and English grammar.

Three years later, in March of 1871, Fukuzawa moved his school to Mita, which remains the primary campus of *Keiô* University today. The Mito school included classes for younger boys between the ages of twelve and sixteen, and by 1874 an elementary school was added also. In 1871, Fukuzawa once again presented corporation agreements stating that the school was a cooperative organization of colleagues in which no one would be superior to anyone else, not even Fukuzawa himself. There were colleagues who taught, and those who learned, and some who did both. Each received a salary for teaching and paid tuition for learning. All members of the corporation were invited to serve in various capacities according to their abilities and, regardless of each one's specified role, all members were invited to express opinions.

The formulation of the school's educational goals, including the Western studies, cooperative operation, and rules of deportment, grew out of Fukuzawa's interpretation of attitudes and ideas he had absorbed from his observations in Western countries and from his idiosyncratic reading of Western texts. Based on his analyses of these sources, he concluded that a fundamental priority of education was to inculcate freedom and independence in students. He was also impressed with the Western ideal of equality. Over the next decades he would write about this peculiarly Western concept extensively and try to work his own version of equality into his educational plan. These social and philosophical qualities, he believed, were important for the students' own intellectual growth and equally important for the development of the new nation of Japan, which was just emerging. He was a firm believer in the the slogan of the era, "**civilization and enlightenment**," a slogan attributed, in fact, to him. Liberal, Western-based ideas would pervade his writing throughout the decade of the 1870s. After that time, he would modify his thinking and express views more in line with a kind of patriotic nationalism that bordered on chauvinism.

IV

"Civilization and Enlightenment"

With the withdrawal of the *shogun* and the defeat of the *bakufu* troops in Edo in the spring of 1868, the way was cleared for the establishment of a new government. The victorious *samurai* from such powerful domains as Satsuma, Chôshu, and Tosa, had already determined that they would base the new central authority on the Kyoto court as personified in the teenaged emperor. The defeat of the House of Tokugawa and the restoration of a legitimate single authority in the heir to the imperial throne was described using a classical Chinese term, **goishin**, or the honorable new beginning. The accepted English translation, "restoration," does not do justice to the creative initiation of institutions that was about to take place. Later that same year, the new emperor would take the reign name of Meiji, and the era of "enlightened rule" would begin. The Meiji Period (1868-1912) was to become more than a mere restoration of imperial authority; it was to be a singular time bound by new institutions with revolutionary overtones.

The slogan "civilization and enlightenment," which captured the spirit of this new era, has been attributed to Fukuzawa Yûkichi. He drew on Western rational thought and theories of national progress that came from French and American sources as he translated books he had acquired from his trips abroad. From his study of Western thinkers, he determined that Japan was just leaving the stage of feudalism and was about to enter

55

the stage of scientific progress characteristic of more advanced civilizations, like those in the West. He believed, then, that both the public and the government of the new Meiji era could aspire to a higher level of enlightened, civilized living through education and absorption of Western ways. He was determined to be a part of this process through his school, writing, and lecturing.

Exactly what shape this new civilization would take was uncertain during Meiji's first decade. Questions abounded in those early years. What would this new Japan be like? Who would actually take charge? Surely it wouldn't be a fifteen-year-old monarch. How would a nation emerge with allegiance to a central authority out of the mishmash of unequal domains, leftover *bakufu* retainers, townspeople and merchants, and peasants in villages and hamlets? It would not appear as if these diverse groups could possibly be served by a single central authority. How would the tangled internal issues of social status, *samurai* stipends, peasant production, government financing, education, strong army, local government, and so forth be resolved? The *bakufu*'s rules had been overturned. Who would make new rules so that peace and stability would return to the country? What would happen to Japan's treaty obligations and, in general, her relations with foreign countries? The victors had based their fight on both "restoring the emperor" and "expelling the foreigner." Would anti-foreignism win the day as well? There was much to be done for a new nation to emerge and for "civilization and enlightenment" to take hold. Just what shape that new Japan would take was unknown in 1868.

A New Circle of Power

Samurai from Satsuma, Chôshu, Tosa, and other powerful domains quickly took over the reins of government when they saw their side was headed toward an easy victory. They issued policy statements that outlined the form the new government would take, much in the manner that the old *bakufu* had put up notices announcing new laws. These *samurai*, soon to be described as a governing **oligarchy**, legitimized their actions by issuing documents in the name of the emperor. This began in

April 1868 with a proclamation known as the **Charter Oath**. This document, ostensibly written by the emperor, outlined the governmental and social foundations of the new nation. In fact, the final version of five articles was the one revised by Kido Takayoshi, a *samurai* of Chôshu. The oath called for an assembly of *daimyô* in which decisions would be made after open discussion; "the high and the low" (*samurai* and commoners) to administer together financial affairs; both military and "common people" to be allowed to fulfill their goals without strife; past evil practices to be abandoned and accepted world precepts followed; and, finally, knowledge to be sought worldwide to strengthen the foundation of imperial rule.

Immediately after the Charter Oath was proclaimed by the emperor, the new oligarchy, which was dominated by the antiforeign *shishi samurai* from Satsuma and Chôshu, issued a fistful of ordinances and regulations. They established a **Council of State**, which had a Western-inspired apparent separation of powers between legislative, executive, and judicial powers; called for qualified men selected by cities, domains, and prefectures to become participants; and set up a taxation system covering all of the status groups within the traditional four classes. In a less formal manner, laws to control the common people were fastened to notice boards pounded into the ground, just as they had been under the Tokugawa *bakufu*. Such laws included the prohibition of murder, arson, and robbery, as one would expect, but also contained the admonition to perform moral and compassionate acts. Surprisingly, given the anti-foreign leanings of those in charge, some of the notice boards declared that the **Imperial Court** intended to honor foreign commitments and therefore no one should harm a foreigner or commit an act that cause an international crisis. The slogan of the civil war, "repel the foreigner," was no longer an accepted sentiment. All of the declarations, ordinances, and new laws were written by members of the oligarchy and issued in the name of His Imperial Majesty.

From 1869 to 1873, the oligarchy, in the name of the emperor, skillfully managed to implement significant changes in the political, economic, and social systems of Japan. Within these few years, the domains were abolished, to be replaced by prefectural governments with allegiance to the central authority. Perhaps more importantly, these prefectures paid their taxes to the new central government in the capital, now called Tokyo. The four classes of the Tokugawa (*samurai*, peasant, artisan, and merchant), and their various subcategories, were abolished; and new classifications were eventually whittled down to just two, aristocrats and common people. Intermarriage between these two classes was permitted. The outcasts, who were beneath all of the other classes, were made full citizens within the much larger class of commoners. On the other hand, a new unofficial privileged class was quickly moving to the fore, that of the government official. The majority of ex-*samurai* proved to be a great financial burden on the new central government. Consequently, their stipends were reduced almost immediately, and then, in 1876, commuted to pensions in the form of bonds. Unfortunately, due to limited national financial resources, the old class of lower-ranking *samurai*, like Fukuzawa, realized very little recompense from these bonds.

By 1872 the peasant farmers could purchase their land and become independent farmers, but, because they were taxed in cash, they suffered mightily from this change. Uprisings by peasants protesting their impoverished circumstances broke out throughout the country, with the last one occurring in 1884. One would be justified in claiming that it was on the backs of the peasants that the government built its programs as it attempted to modernize and westernize Japan. Other changes implemented in a few short years included universal education, conscription of commoners for the new army, establishment of a central police system, underwriting some industrialization, and modernizing transportation and communication systems. Throughout the decade of the 1870s, as the new Meiji leaders created new institutions, modified them, and called for yet more public sacrifice, they sustained criticism, opposition, sometimes violent uprisings, and even military conflict, but in the end, somehow the perspective of this small group of young men prevailed.

Fukuzawa (second from left) and Keiô students, 1874. Third from left is Nakamigawa Hikojirô, Fukuzawa's nephew, whom Fukuzawa sent to England to be educated. (Courtesy of Keiô University.)

Fukuzawa's Response to the Meiji Government

At the same time that the emperor proclaimed his Charter Oath, as instructed by his circle of advisors, Fukuzawa successfully opened his new school, *Keiô Gijuku*. The financing for this venture came from the royalties from the sale of the first two volumes of *Conditions in the West*. The reception of his publications had been extraordinary, indicating that many of his countrymen on both sides of the civil conflict were eager to learn more about the West. In fact, some parts of the Charter Oath, according to one of its drafters, were influenced by Fukuzawa's writings about Western government. There was no doubt that Fukuzawa had done well to keep himself above the fray, out of the way of bullets and swords, and, in fact, productive during the chaotic months that saw the demise of the Tokugawa *bakufu*. Given the recognized need for knowledge from the West, the implicit need for educated leaders, and the obvious need for practical and scientific learning, it would seem self-evident that Fukuzawa would be called upon to serve in the new government. After all, he was credited with two of the best known slogans that characterized the mood of the period, *bunmei kaika* (civilization and enlightenment) and *fukoku kyōhei* (rich nation, strong army), and he was a noted translator of things Western. Surely he would have a contribution to make to the new government.

Indeed, in June 1868, when the new government set up temporary offices in both Osaka and Edo, several *bakufu* translators, including Fukuzawa, were "ordered" to join the new offices. Fukuzawa was told to come to Osaka. He refused, saying that he was "ill." After the government moved to Edo, he was asked once again to join, and once again he refused. One of his friends, who had answered the first call, reprimanded him and urged him to enter into government service. Fukuzawa responded adamantly that he did not "like the service" and implied that he should be admired just as much for choosing to reject the call as the friend was for accepting it. He was asked a few more times to go into public service. One such request would have made him the bureaucrat in charge of the nation's schooling, but Fukuzawa wanted to remain independent. He declined every government invitation. He stated in his autobiography that his refusal was based on the belief that the new government would continue its anti-foreign line and that he could not be associated with such a policy. He further commented, from his late-century perspective, that, fortunately, he had been wrong and that "the government gradually turned to liberalism, bringing on the fine development we see today [1899]."

Fukuzawa was less than candid about his refusal to join the government. He, like his friends, had been asked to work as a translator, a role suitable to a minor bureaucrat with no political power. By this time, several of Fukuzawa's associates, who had also served the *bakufu* at its **Institute for the Study of Barbarian Books**, had joined the new government as translators and researchers. Fukuzawa believed, however, that he had outgrown translation work, with the exception, of course, of his lucrative private jobs. In the next few years he even turned down private commissions and declared that he would no longer do translation at all. The Fukuzawa scholar Professor Norio Tamaki also discounts Fukuzawa's excuse that government service would align Fukuzawa with anti-foreign policies. Tamaki suggests that Fukuzawa was much too well informed about domain missions to the West and the growing general interest in things Western to believe that "repel the foreigner" could be any more than a slogan for gaining power. One might add that Fukuzawa was less than candid when he stated in 1899 that he believed the fledgling Meiji government was turning toward Western liberalism. He was only too aware of the vehement arguments among powerful ex-*samurai* within the government in the late 1860s and early 1870s over the direction the nation should take to make such a simplistic analysis. And, finally, we can't take him at his word as he reflected on those early government years, because he, too, changed his interpretation over the next several decades about both the meaning of "liberalism" and the direction of "fine development" which he claimed the government had followed.

Perhaps more to the point, however, is the fact that during 1868-69, Fukuzawa's private enterprises were proceeding very successfully. He was pleased with the development of *Keiô Gijuku* under his sole management, and he was doing well financially from his other endeavors. He would have seen a government job as a demotion in influence and salary as well as a surrender of his independence. Instead of spending time in public service, Fukuzawa looked forward to adding more money-making businesses to his resume. For example, when he realized that his book *On Conditions in the West* had sold so many copies, and that several other books he had written or translated on Western military, science, and government had also sold well, he began to begrudge the amount of profit he was losing through publication costs. To remedy this situation, he bought a huge supply of paper wholesale, hired some artisans, and set out to do his own publishing. Thus he moved from merely writing the manuscript to publishing and selling it. This meant he controlled the entire production of a book from "copying the manuscript, cutting the wood block (which is cut by hand from the copy pasted on the block), making the prints from the block, and binding the sheets," to introducing his work and selling it. His royalties increased, as did his interest in the publishing business. Later he would brag that he made more money than high officials did. Why, then, would he want to join the government? He was becoming influential in his own right, and he was maintaining his independence and freedom, two concepts he valued highly and would write about extensively over the next years.

Western Enlightenment

During the 1860s, the *bakufu* and several of the domains each sent missions to Europe primarily, but also to America. Their goal was to learn the secret of the West's scientific and military successes. It had become obvious to both *bakufu* and *han* officials that, if Japan were to advance to a point at which she could throw off the yoke of unequal treaties, legal subservience, and commercial inferiority, her citizens would need to absorb Western learning. And so, in addition to the formal missions, a number of young men were sent to London, Paris, Berlin, and other major cities for a year or more to study science, medicine, engineering, ethics, philosophy, and so forth. After the Meiji Restoration, the new government continued to send people to the West in search of "enlightenment" and "civilization" as it sought to uncover the secrets of Western military strength and economic riches.

The famous 1871 Iwakura Mission was led by Iwakura Tomomi and included forty-nine officials, one of whom was Kido Takayoshi, who had authored the Charter Oath. Two other well-known oligarchs who accompanied the group were Itô Hirobumi, who would one day become Prime Minister, and Okubo Toshimichi. These two men were greatly influenced by a meeting with the Chancellor of the new German state, Otto von Bismarck. who impressed upon them the need to encourage patriotism in their citizens and economic and military strength in their government. Also in the group were fifty-two male students and five young girls who traveled and studied in Europe and America. Seven-year-old Tsuda Ume would remain in Washington, D.C., for eleven years and later return to the U.S. a second time to attend and graduate from Bryn Mawr College in Philadelphia. In 1900 she would found a girls' school, the present-day Tsuda Women's College of Tokyo.

Also, during the 1860s and early 1870s Western writings in scientific, political, philosophical, and cultural fields were imported into Japan, and translators like Fukuzawa provided the public with their versions of these European and American thinkers. For example, Fukuzawa freely translated, including his own additions and subtractions, the works of F. Wayland, noted conservative American ethicist and president of Brown University; H.T. Buckle, historian, of England; and F. P. G. Guizot, French historian of Western civilization, among others. Nakamura Masanao, a colleague of Fukuzawa, who had also refused to serve in the new government, translated the most widely read foreign book, *Self-Help* by the Englishman Samuel Smiles, and the influential work *On Liberty*, by J. S. Mill. These were just a few of the writers who influenced the substantial group of literate Japanese eager to abandon their unprogressive ways. Later, works by more Western thinkers were brought to Japan, including those of Herbert Spencer, Jean-Jacques Rousseau, and Charles Darwin. These did not necessarily appear in print in the order in which the authors lived and wrote.

Fukuzawa Yûkichi was one of early Meiji's most prolific translators, but he felt free to augment the works he translated. He wrote original pieces based on his interpretation of Western thought and colored by his pre-restoration attitudes and experiences. An original work, considered to be one of his most popular and influential writings, was *Gakumon no susume*, known in English as *An Encouragement of Learning* or *An Invitation to Learning*. This work was published in 17 sections, or pamphlets, between 1872 and 1876. Most of the essays were written in a style easy for the reading public to grasp, using common Japanese characters (*kanji*) with which a non-scholar would be familiar. To further enlighten his readers, he introduced the new Western concepts over and over again and illustrated the explanations with descriptive stories. The concepts were so alien to Japanese experience that Fukuzawa had to coin new words and reinterpret old ones to present these foreign ideas. The final result was never identical to the Western model and sometimes significantly different. The first essay in this series was originally written as a lecture Fukuzawa gave in his hometown of Nakatsu. The occasion was the establishment of Nakatsu's first post-restoration school. He had been invited to speak by Okudaira Masayuki, the *daimyô*, then governor, who declared that the school was to be for "all people in the new prefecture, whether *samurai* or commoner, and also older and accomplished citizens, too" who might want to improve themselves and engage in Western studies (Kiyooka, 1985). Fukuzawa was encouraged to publish his lecture. It sold well in pamphlet form, and other schools also began to use it as a teaching text. Soon it became so popular that some of the ideas expressed in the pamphlet were incorporated into the 1872 Education Act, which established state run schools with a four-year compulsory education requirement.

This first essay in *An Encouragement of Learning* began:

> "Heaven never created a man above another nor a man below another," it is said. Therefore, when people are born, Heaven's idea is that all should be equal to all others without distinction of high and low or noble and mean, and they should all work with their bodies and minds with a dignity deserving of the lords of creation, which they are, and make use of all things in the world to satisfy their needs in clothing, food, and dwelling, freely but without interfering with others, each to live happily through life. (Translated by Kiyooka, 1985.)

It will be remembered that the inequality in the Tokugawa status system had angered Fukuzawa from his childhood days. He did not need Western thinkers to tell him that hereditary distinctions between people, especially those applied to *samurai*, were immoral, but he appreciated the support of their scholarship as he sought to draw his readers away from *bakufu*-established hierarchies. On the other hand, Fukuzawa did not believe in a creator god in the Western sense, and so he drew upon his own culture and inserted a word that could be translated

"Heaven" to solve this problem. The pamphlet continued with the observation that, although equality is the natural state of man, this does not mean there are no differences among people in intellect, ability, or wealth. These differences, however, Fukuzawa declared, were not inherent but resulted from differences in education.

There is more to his tale, however. Not just any sort of education would make individuals wise, wealthy, and successful. After all, people were educated under the *bakufu* and, in fact, for many years before that. Traditional Japanese education, however, was based on Confucianism, which venerated the Chinese classics and "ancient and difficult literature" and the writing of poetry. These accomplishments might have been good for learned scholars but were hardly practical for everyday employment in commerce, medicine, politics, business, farming, or any other occupation of importance to the advancement of civilization. Practical studies (based on Western models, of course), which included mathematics, physics, geography, weights and measures, history, and ethics, were what was needed to educate the individual and enrich the nation. And here, Fukuzawa explained what he meant by equality, freedom, and independence. "The nature of a human being at birth is not bound or restricted; men and women as adults should be free and unrestrained in their actions." Everyone is equal at birth and free and independent as an adult; however, freedom must include restraint based on each individual's limitations, or one is likely "to fall into waywardness and licentiousness." How does one determine proper actions and appropriate restraint? One should "conform to the reasons of Heaven and humanity" and attain personal freedom "without infringing upon that of others." Individual freedom and independence are fundamental; and wealth, success, and wisdom will accrue to those who pursue a practical education based on Western models. But one must follow guidance from Heaven (the government) and do nothing (uprisings, revolution) to disrupt the freedom of others. On a grander scale, the nation should be free within the community of the world and, should any other nation attempt to restrain Japan, thereby placing her freedom in jeopardy, each citizen should fight, "even at the risk of his own life" for the nation's Heaven-bestowed freedom.

This essay was embraced by the new Ministry of Education for several reasons. First, while it venerated individual freedom and independence, possibly a frightening prospect for the government, it praised the current officials for their enlightenment. Fukuzawa illustrated the new government's progress by referring to the abolition of such "miserable laws and customs" as the compulsory separation of the classes. Second, the essay underscored that both the citizen and the nation should grow in wisdom and independence. This was a community of citizens working together for the advancement of the nation. If both citizens and nation acted unselfishly, and if the citizens of the nation used their education in principled and moral ways and thus achieved personal dignity and success, their government would prosper, and officials would be obliged to rule with fairness and justice. And, he suggested, this was exactly what had happened so far. However, he warned, if the people acted foolishly and became "lazy and licentious" the government would have to use force to restore the appropriate relationship between nation and citizens. It is clear that even during those early years of Meiji, when Fukuzawa was at his most liberal, Confucian thought lingered behind his words. The oligarchy must have breathed a sigh of relief when they read his words that restraining actions by the government would not indicate that it was despotic but, rather, that foolish people had brought the government's restrictions upon themselves. As this pamphlet showed, Fukuzawa mixed together his own versions of individualism and nationalism, independence and restraint, and political liberalism and conservatism.

The other sixteen essays in *An Encouragement of Learning,* which were published at irregular intervals until 1876, reiterated the themes presented in the first essay, as well as introducing new ideas about morality, education, rule of law, representative government, taxation, equality between men and women, and other Western ideas and institutions. For example, in the second essay Fukuzawa spoke of the importance of learning "letters," that is, Japanese characters (*kanji*), a difficult and time-consuming discipline necessary to learning to read Japanese. He said, "Letters (*kanji*) are the instruments of learning. They are like the hammers and saws used to build a house"(translated in Dilworth and Hirano). But then, continuing with his concrete comparison, he argued that one who knows the names of tools but does not know how to use them "cannot be called a carpenter." Similarly, he noted, one who knows Japanese characters (*kanji*) but cannot understand the principles they are used to represent does not really know how to read.

In other essays Fukuzawa supported the right of the government to make laws and to enforce them, including the right to impose punishments. However, he insisted, citizens could avoid the establishment of tyrannical government by pursuing learning with the intention of knowledgeably influencing officials. Here he suggested that some sort of representative government would be appropriate. He applied his concept of equality to nations as well as individuals. He insisted that all nations were inherently equal but noted that some nations, like England and France, were stronger than others, like Japan. However, as in the case of individuals, the stronger nations should not prey upon the weaker ones. He also believed in the natural upward progression of civilization. Thus a weak but advancing nation like Japan could rise to the level attained by powerful Western nations through study, practical application of learning, and hard work on the part of its officials and citizens.

A Journal of "Enlightenment"

Fukuzawa was not the only Japanese who sought Western-style "civilization and enlightenment" for Meiji Japan. Another, Mori Arinori, an official member of Japan's first embassy in Washington, D.C., returned from America in 1873 enthusiastic about forming a scholarly society similar to what he had observed in the West. Among the men he gathered together to form the **Meiji Six Society** in the sixth year of Meiji were Fukuzawa, his associate in translation; Nakamura Masanao; Katô Hiroyuki; and six others. Later these were joined by eighteen more men, including one foreigner, the American educator W. E. Griffis. The group met regularly at a restaurant in Tokyo to discuss the issues of the day, and several of them contributed articles to the *Meiji Six Journal*, thus exposing their debates to a wider audience. Journal contributions ran the gamut from discussions of whether scholars should take up official government positions, an issue especially dear to Fukuzawa, to descriptions of ways to honor the emperor by casting out barbaric customs, as opposed to the Western barbarians themselves.

Women were discussed under topics such as wives and concubines, equality of husbands and wives, and the elimination of prostitution. Several articles contained translations and philosophical discussion of foreign words and phrases such as *liberty*, *freedom*, *civilization*, and *natural rights*. European theories of philosophy such as the Frenchman Auguste Comte's positivism and the Englishman Jeremy Bentham's utilitarianism, were explained. There were discussions of Western and Japanese religion, government, military, and law, including punishment, capital punishment, and torture. Financial topics included trade balance, use of paper currency, speculation, taxation, and free trade. All in all, this journal made it clear that the early 1870s was an exciting time intellectually and politically. The structure of the new Japan, including its social, political, and economic institutions, was yet to be determined; and even the matter of who, in the end, would make such decisions was far from clear. Therefore, every topic that affected the "civilizing" of Japan, its relationship with the West, or the "enlightenment" of its people was worthy of debate; and there was always someone in the group ready to support or decry every position on any question.

Fukuzawa did not contribute as many articles as some of his associates, but, as one of the six directors of the Meiji Six Society, he participated in group decisions; and his perspective on issues was at least tacitly acknowledged by his Meiji Six colleagues. Sometimes other Meiji Six writers responded in the journal to Fukuzawa's thinking as expressed in his *Invitation to Learning* essays and in *Keiô Gijuku*'s publication, *People's Journal*. For Fukuzawa followed his own advice and protected his independence and freedom by speaking and writing in many different forums. In most cases, he favored those media that he could control. Just the same, as one of the most recognized personalities of the 1870s, Fukuzawa was courted by the other members of the Meiji Six Society, who both listened and responded to what he had to say.

Three debates in which Fukuzawa figured prominently were government service, representative government, and various issues related to women. In the first instance, Fukuzawa wrote in the fourth of his essays, in *An Encouragement of Learning*, that scholars should stay out of government service. His argument was unflattering even toward the scholars in the Meiji Six Society, most of whom had become government officials. He said of these people that they had been "nurtured by their education, to have eyes for official positions, believing that no worthwhile work can be accomplished except through the government" (trans. in Kiyooka). And yet, he insisted, these scholars did not really understand the role of either the government or its citizens. Furthermore, Fukuzawa believed that greater advancement was needed in the private sector if Japan's civilization was to progress and her independence to be secured. Good minds were needed outside of government to establish commerce, promote trade, and run factories; and these accomplishments should be achieved independently of government sanction. Those in official positions, he said, were often flattered into making decisions favored by particular groups. And certain citizens had begun to depend upon the patronage that accrued to an official's followers. He observed that Western scholars who had become officials soon fell into a pit of insincerity and falsehood as they followed the trail of favor and advantage pressed upon them by those who hoped to use those in high places for personal and business gain. On the other hand, flattering himself while making his point, Fukuzawa suggested that many of the national changes recently achieved were first advocated directly or indirectly by himself, a private citizen. He was proud that by teaching and demonstrating he was able to promote new ideas, something he believed was not possible within government circles.

Fukuzawa's *Meiji Six Journal* associates were unhappy with his article on government service and dedicated their second issue to critical responses by four Society members. Katô Hiroyuki, one of the more conservative members of the Society and a government official, objected to what he saw as Fukuzawa's bias in favor of the private sector. National development, he argued, should proceed through the public actions of those in government rather than through the efforts of private individuals. Furthermore, it was the duty of intellectuals, such as Fukuzawa, to join the government for the good of the nation. Katô also criticized Japan's new political parties and, by implication, Fukuzawa himself for taking the ideas of freedom and independence too far.

Mori Arinori used Western logic to take apart Fukuzawa's arguments and, while calling him an "honorable friend," ridiculed Fukuzawa for arguing that official service could not be as profitable to society as private service. He went on to criticize Fukuzawa for implying that the nation would progress only after the scholars had left government "entirely to the unlettered." All of the responses by Society members acknowledged that authoritarianism, factionalism, and cronyism, underlying themes in Fukuzawa's comments, were worrisome in any government. But they also insisted that scholars could play a positive role in Japan's modern progress toward civilization and enlightenment through performance in either the public or the private sector. Fukuzawa remained unconvinced, and the debate continued.

A second important debate aired in the *Meiji Six Journal* focused on representative government. General discussion of this issue had begun with the issuance of the Charter Oath of 1868, for many Japanese believed that the "assembly" mentioned in this proclamation was to be some sort of parliament. The general argument in favor of and against representative government continued with great vigor, and even violence at times, until a constitution was promulgated by the emperor in 1889. In the 1870s this debate was just getting started. Various members of the Meiji Six Society held each of the positions fought over in the larger community. Katô Hiroyuki, for example, believed that peasants and townsmen were too stupid to participate in elections, and so the citizenry was not yet ready for any sort of representative government. Fukuzawa; his fellow translator of

Western writings, Nakamura Masanao; and others refuted Katô, saying that, given appropriate voting restrictions, some sort of representative body could be formed. Fukuzawa was particularly offended by Katô's perspective and explained, "Those who imagine fools they do not see are as foolish as the fools they imagine" (Braisted). Although Fukuzawa agreed that the uneducated, like tenant farmers and ricksha drivers, could not be expected to participate in government, he assured the journal's readers that the people he classified as educated "middle class" could easily participate in an assembly. He looked forward to such an institution becoming a debating society. Other Meiji Six members wanted an assembly but one appointed by those in high office. This discussion contained within it a debate over popular rights and the struggle for the establishment of party politics that would play out during the next decade. Finally, in 1890, a constitutionally established bicameral parliament, with a house of representatives elected by a limited group of male taxpayers, would be seated.

Fukuzawa had been formulating a view of women's rights for many years, and this issue also concerned some of the others within the Meiji Six Society. One aspect of this third broad discussion concerned the roles of wives and concubines within a family. Both by example and through debate, Fukuzawa made it clear that he believed a marriage should be monogamous and that he did not support the taking of concubines. In the eighth essay of *An Encouragement of Learning* Fukuzawa reported that many men contended that if they could treat all of their wives, that is, their primary wife and any concubines, properly, and if they could support them all equally, then why should anyone object? He queried back, what would men think if women were allowed to support many husbands, calling them male concubines, and that these secondary husbands were made to serve in inferior positions in the household? He stated that if the latter situation were acceptable to men, he would quit talking against the system of female concubines. Such facetious bantering aside, Fukuzawa believed that the custom of concubinage was a primary component of barbarism, which was holding back the civilization of the family and thereby the advancement of the nation. On the other hand, he was not looking to revolutionize social custom too quickly. As he commented in the *Meiji Six Journal*, although he believed that equal rights for husbands and wives should be a goal of the new society, it was probably too early to press for such a policy.

Under the title "On Wives and Concubines," Mori Arinori, a Christian, spoke more broadly and resolutely about the immoral Japanese custom of legally sanctioning both an official wife and the purchase of one or more subservient "wives," that is, concubines. In five essays he intertwined the issue of concubines with a discussion of the equality that should prevail between husband and wife in a marriage and the importance of a single wife and mother for the sake of the children. Mori concluded his series with a detailed contract that he felt should be entered into by the prospective husband and wife, which required mutual agreement and mutual rights and duties for husband and wife. When Mori was married in 1875, he and his wife signed an agreement similar to the contract he had proposed, which Fukuzawa witnessed.

The conservative Meiji Six member, Katô Hiroyuki, wrote two essays making fun of the comments on equality between husbands and wives and the condemnation of the system of concubines as presented by both Fukuzawa and Mori. His argument was founded on his belief that modern Europeans had gone too far in providing for equal rights for husbands and wives and that in fact wives seemed to be surpassing their husbands in rights. He then listed several Western customs, which Europeans would have simply called polite etiquette, showing that wives were catered to in seating arrangements, opening of doors, expectation of discreet speech, and so forth. Although he obviously misunderstood the arguments made by his associates, he did complicate the debate substantially when he switched from using the terms *husbands* and *wives* to speaking about equal rights for men and women. Neither Mori nor Fukuzawa were ready to concede that men and women should be given equal rights. They were appalled by Katô's suggestion that they supported equality between men and women outside of marriage and outside of the home. This was, after all, the 1870s, and only the most liberal European philosophers, such as J. S.

Mill, supported equality of women with men. Certainly no Western government had granted equal rights.

Discussion of these topics and others would come to an end as far as the Meiji Six Society was concerned in 1875. They had been intellectually stimulating, broadly based, widely read, and timely. Perhaps that was their downfall. Seeing the effect discussion of this kind was having on the citizenry, the government decided it was time to assert better management over the content and direction of public debate. Through the auspices of his imperial majesty, the Council that controlled the new government issued press and libel regulations that would hold editors responsible for everything published in their journals. Some in the Meiji Six Society hoped they could continue to write about topics designed to enlighten the public while steering clear of political subjects. Fukuzawa stated flatly that there was no point in continuing the journal under such circumstances, as writers would have to conform to government perspectives. He voted to shut down the journal, just as he had already disbanded the Keiô Gijuku's *People's Journal*. In the end that view prevailed, and the last issue was published in November 1875. The Meiji Six Society did not long survive its journal.

Discussion of crucial issues, however, could not be stopped by government fiat, at least, not yet. Informal groups of men and women joined forces and spoke out throughout the country in defense of the rights of the people. Also, individuals and groups of like-minded peasants and townspeople set up organizations that foreshadowed political parties. Many of these individuals and groups were adamantly opposed to the government in power. It is no wonder, then, that the oligarchy issued regulation upon regulation in an attempt to keep the people in check and thus hold on to power. This would be a good test for Fukuzawa's theories about the actions scholars could take as private citizens to influence government officials. In this censorial climate, could people like Fukuzawa and his Meiji Six Society colleagues encourage the oligarchs and their appointed bureaucrats to make decisions that would further the nation along the path of "civilization and enlightenment"?

Fukuzawa and Popular Rights

Mita Debating Hall as it still stands on *Keiô* University grounds.
(H. Hopper, 2001.)

The small group of high officials who dominated the fledgling Meiji government drew up many regulations in their first five years of power. Their power to make law in the name of the emperor seemed to make them supreme. Fukuzawa had been very clever not to be drawn into the lowly position that his previous service for the *bakufu* and his membership in the Nakatsu-*han* might have secured for him. There was little possibility that he could have risen to a level competitive with the powerful clique that had assumed the leadership of the new government. As things turned out, however, by the time the first decade of the Meiji era came to a close, Fukuzawa Yûkichi's name was well known to the public, and he had become a person of influence with several of the most powerful leaders in the Meiji government. His acclaim among the reading public and his ability to bring pressure upon those in high office would only increase in the 1880s and 1890s. As he had argued so eloquently, political power did not reside only with those holding public office. In fact, several of the victorious *samurai* who held significant power at the beginning of Meiji were gone in both office and influence by the middle of the 1870s, while Fukuzawa's name was sounded loud and often through his publications, speeches, and influential conversations behind the scenes.

A part of Fukuzawa's acclaim was due to his introduction to his compatriots of the Western practice of speech making and debate. During Meiji Six Society meetings, he had argued vehemently against those of his colleagues who believed that the Japanese did not have the ability or a language adequately complex to discuss matters of importance in a public forum. Fukuzawa insisted that both the Japanese language and the character of the people were suited for expressing ideas publicly before an audience. He coined a Japanese word, *enzetsu*, which stood for the English term *speech*. He then made public speaking a subject within his school's curriculum, and he himself practiced that art through a debating society that he organized in 1874. In 1875, he built a home for this organization, the Mita Debating Hall, which has been preserved on the Keiô University campus. In addition, Fukuzawa published books on the practices of public speaking, presiding over meetings, and debating. These writings not only described the process of organizing meetings and presenting ideas before an audience, but discussed the usefulness of speeches and debates in conveying information. He also explained the role of the audience. Public speaking and debate soon became a new mode of communication for Fukuzawa, and thus a new medium of influence. He was determined, however, to inspire others to join him in this Western practice, and he was so successful in this endeavor that speaking before an audience soon became an accepted way of disseminating political ideas. The Meiji oligarchs saw that they could be easily challenged through public speeches and debates and, given the shakiness of their hold on power in the 1870s, the Council of State promulgated additional laws designed to stifle the public's new voice. They found that nothing they did, however, could put out the fires of debate, either within their small clique or among the citizenry at large.

Civil Strife

In 1873, the Iwakura Mission to Europe and America returned home eager to share what they had learned with fellow members of the ruling oligarchy. Instead, they found themselves embroiled in heated discussions about domestic and foreign policies. Soon, in fact, some members of the Satsuma-Chôshu-Tosa clique, which had controlled the government since the downfall of the *bakufu*, would withdraw from government service. One immediate cause of contention was the apparent snub by the Korean government, which had refused to kowtow to Japan's Western-style diplomatic demands. There was heated debate within the Meiji Council of State as to whether to send an expedition to force the Korean government to respond in the same way that Western embassies had required of Japan in the 1850s.

Another conflict which greeted the returning officials, Okubo Toshimichi, Iwakura Tomomi, Itô Hirobumi, and Kido Takayoshi, concerned their fellow *samurai*. They found that in their absence certain other Council members, also ex-*samurai* from western *han*, had expressed anger over recent laws that stripped the *samurai* class of its privileges and decreased individual stipends. Furthermore, the returned Council members found their associates arguing about what form the new government should take. Some leaders wanted a written constitution along Western lines; others were afraid that might limit their own power. Some endorsed an assembly with limited legislative powers, as had been promised by the Charter Oath of 1868; others felt the citizenry was not advanced enough to take on such responsibility.

A few leaders resigned from the Council in protest over these political quarrels and founded political action groups to mobilize public opinion. In this way they hoped to establish a base of power to fight against policies to which they objected. Two of these heavily disputed changes were the new compulsory education system and military conscription, both of which had met with negative public reaction. All in all, the Iwakura Mission officials, who had expected upon their return to apply newly learned Western approaches to the modernization of their nation, unexpectedly found themselves engaged in debate over internal and foreign issues. In 1873, no one could predict with certainty whether these quarrels would end peacefully or through military action, nor was it clear which individuals or groups would come out on top in the expected power struggle.

Saigô Takamori from Satsuma, a hero of the civil war, led the most violent, if brief, challenge that government leaders had to face. A leading Council member, Saigô pressed his proposal to send an expeditionary force to Korea. He wanted to punish the Korean government for its insulting rejection of Japan's diplomatic instruction that Korea enter into an agreement with Japan similar to her unequal treaties with the West. More important than the foreign relations aspect of this proposal, however, was its internal ramifications. Saigô saw such a mission as an opportunity to employ and pay the many disillusioned and impoverished *samurai*. Fukuzawa weighed in on this argument from the sidelines in opposition to Saigô's plan of foreign intrusion. Since Fukuzawa had voluntarily surrendered his stipend at the beginning of the new era, he had no inclination to support Saigô's *samurai* aid package either. Because Fukuzawa was only beginning to make a name for himself, however, more important opposition at this time came from other members of the ruling Council. Okubo, Itô, and Iwakura, who believed that Japan was not yet economically or militarily strong enough to engage in an overseas military action, spoke out against Saigô's plan.

Dismayed by the rebuff of his fellow Council members, Saigô left the government in disgust. He returned to his home in Kagoshima on Kyushu to farm. Other former Satsuma *samurai* were not as accepting of the government's refusal to take up arms. By 1877, these Satsuma ex-*samurai* had formed an army, rounded up an arsenal of weapons, and convinced Saigô to lead them into battle against the government. This insurrection was bloody, counting more dead and wounded than the whole of the "restoration" struggle, but, thankfully, it was also brief. The Satsuma rebels never made it out of Kyushu. They were defeated by an army of conscripts headed by Saigô's old military ally and colleague in government, Yamagata Aritomo. The Satsuma Rebellion of 1877 ended in Saigô's death. The oligarchy had met this military challenge and won, but at great human and economic cost. In fact, the government's treasury would suffer for several years to come as a result of the expense of this second civil war. Fukuzawa, too, would feel the cost as operations at his school would begin to falter for lack of support and money, an effect directly attributed to the war.

Stifling Free Speech and Free Press

Another ex-member of the ruling oligarchy, Itagaki Taisuke, formerly a *samurai* of the Tosa *han*, also left the Council and returned home over the Korea issue. However, he went to work immediately to gain support for a national assembly that would counterbalance the power of the oligarchs. In 1874, he petitioned the ruling Council, his ex-colleagues, demanding that they permit the establishment of a governing body that would be chosen by the people. More alarming to the Council than his demand was the fact that he published his petition in newspapers, exposing his verbal attack on government tyranny to a broad audience. Itagaki formed an organization, a forerunner to political parties, to pressure the government to respond to his demands. His ideas caught fire throughout urban and rural Japan because they were printed in newspapers and pamphlets. He gave lectures that attracted men and women from many segments of the society, including farmers, ex-*samurai*, workers, and merchants. The oligarchy believed their control of the public was under threat and decided they must respond. At first they cajoled Itagaki into rejoining the government by promising a gradual move toward, first, local assemblies, and later a national assembly. He was fooled briefly, but soon he again walked away from government service and pressed his cause for immediate change with even greater intensity.

The Council members believed they had to act immediately, decisively, and forcefully if they were to successfully confront growing political threats. First the Council added a new cabinet department, the **Home Ministry**, along dictatorial lines they had observed in some European countries. Okubo Toshimichi was appointed the new Home Minister and thus became, until his assassination by Saigô followers in 1878, commander of the central police force. He was powerful and autocratic, stating "that a strong authoritarian government . . . [would best] serve as the vehicle for prompt execution of decisions" and that "democratic representative government was not suitable to the customs and needs of Japan" (Mitchell). Next, the Council members issued censorship regulations following French legal examples. They were determined to protect their power over public information by stanching the agitation for rights, equality, and representative government caused by books, newspapers, and lectures. The first **press laws** were issued in 1875. These would be strengthened through amendments and the addition of new laws until the end of World War II.

These first censorship laws caused animated debate within the Meiji Six Society. As we have seen, Fukuzawa, having concluded that the society members could not write freely in this atmosphere, spoke in favor of ceasing all publication, which the members agreed to in 1875. Considering that almost all of the journal authors except Fukuzawa were government officials and that the discussions featured in the journal were, at most, only mildly negative toward the government, one can gauge how threatening these laws seemed to publishers of admittedly anti-government newspapers and magazines. The heart of the first Press Ordinances was the requirement that publishers petition the Home Ministry for the right to publish and that they must follow a list of regulations about the nature of permitted publication topics. Moreover, publishers must accept responsibility for anything that appeared in their periodicals. Other ordinances issued at the same time included laws governing book censorship and imprecisely defined libel laws. The vague wording of these laws suggested that publishers and authors could be fined and imprisoned almost at will and that publications could be censored or banned entirely. Simply the threat of government action, as the demise of the moderate *Meiji Six Journal* proved, was enough to bring several publishers into line. On the other hand, the most determined critics of the government refused to given in. One resolute publisher even wrote a condemnatory editorial against the press laws themselves. He was fined and sentenced to prison but let off with house arrest by a sympathetic judge. Other courageous journalists and publishers fought the oligarchy by continuing to cover speeches and writings of people's rights sympathizers. The oligarchy discovered, at least for the time being, that they could not put out all of the democratic fires.

Fukuzawa Discusses Civil Rights and Responsibilities

Fukuzawa had voted to shut down the *Meiji Six Journal* rather than either capitulate to the authorities' press regulations or suffer the consequences of confronting these. On the other hand, he continued to publish books without prejudice. In 1875 he published his most highly acclaimed work, *An Outline of a Theory of Civilization*, which he had finished the year before. Once again, he experienced good sales, though no work would ever reach the heights of his first publication, *An Invitation to Learning*. Although the press laws included regulations on books, Fukuzawa was not harassed by the Home Ministry. This latest book contained details about Western civilizations, mostly selected from the French historian Guizot and the English historian Buckle, and included Fukuzawa's own interpretation of Japanese history. He also delved more deeply into themes he had previously introduced, including issues of national independence, the progressive nature of civilization, the importance of education, and the distinction between knowledge and virtue. In addition, there were a few comments about the political questions that were causing the government so much grief. As was often the case, Fukuzawa positioned himself as critical of both conservative and liberal political camps and couched relevant arguments in a tone that sought consensus.

Fukuzawa noted that in the mid-1870s, there were "few men of intellectual talent" left among the conservative camps and agreed that the "reformist ranks deserv[ed] to increase." Furthermore, he speculated about how the government, be it conservative or reformist, would learn about the needs the people. In order for Japan to advance along the progressive path to civilization, some accounting of the people's requirements would have to be ascertained. The answer to his concerns, he believed, lay in a government composed of intelligent leaders with the talent and willingness to "find out the actual mood of the times." Fukuzawa posited that this goal could best be achieved by "allowing freedom of the press and listening to the opinions of learned men." The alternative, he argued, would be devastating. "Restriction of freedom of the press, obstructing the flow of intelligent ideas, and employing secret agents to observe the mood of the country is like sealing a living thing in an airtight compartment and standing by to watch it die a slow death."

Fukuzawa criticized decisions made by Japan's current leadership. "[O]fficialdom enjoys the greatest concentration of our nation's intellectual talent. But the policies they work out in concert are not by any means the most intelligent." How could this outcome be changed? Here Fukuzawa looked to Western examples. He argued that often government leadership abroad was not as talented as that in Japan. However, through a process of "group consensus," drawn from discussions in parliament; business, religious and academic groups; and even groups in the most remote villages, a "national opinion" could be formulated that would give strength to the country as a whole. Fukuzawa did voice some reservations about his own promotion of agreement by consensus. He admitted that public opinion formed by "unintelligent people" would not help government make good decisions, and, if such were the case, "despotic rule" would be necessary. Public opinion, then, could be enlightening only if the public in question were educated. A society had to be on guard against the opinions of a group dominated by ignorant individuals who argued from selfish perspectives. An example of this, he believed, was the case posed by ex-*samurai* demanding to retain their stipends. Unenlightened opinions such as this one, he argued, proved his theory that public discussion did not always obtain desirable results.

Although *An Outline of a Theory of Civilization* was published in 1875, after the first press laws had been issued, it had been written in 1874. Therefore, it clearly preceded the establishment of the Home Ministry, central police force, and censorship and libel laws. Just the same, this book was subject to the new laws, and so it is instructive that Fukuzawa experienced no official sanctions. Perhaps his writings in the mid-1870s contained just enough praise of Japan's leaders to provide a smoke screen for the critical remarks he made. Or perhaps his ability to criticize both sides of an issue helped to shield him from censorship. Even during the mid-1870s, when Fukuzawa was at his most liberal, he still stressed knowledge, education, independence, and economic success over public rights. Five years later, when he became a successful newspaper publisher, he would experience the consequences of press laws, even though by that time he had become more conservative.

The Movement for Freedom and Popular Rights

Undoubtedly the most significant anti-government political activism of early Meiji took place within the various groups that used the slogan "freedom and popular rights (*jiyû minken*)." It was a broad-based movement that incorporated within its many different configurations and perspectives of men and women, peasants and townspeople, intellectuals and the uneducated, ex-government officials and aspiring politicians. Judging from the reaction of the ruling elite, this movement constituted the greatest threat to their power since the restoration. According to the Japanese scholar Irokawa Daikichi, Fukuzawa's book *An Encouragement of Learning* was a primary catalyst for the thinking of the leaders of the freedom and popular rights groups. This is not surprising given his discussion in that work and other writings, including *Theory of Civilization*, of concepts such as freedom, independence, fundamental rights, responsibility, intelligent leadership, and so forth as well as his clearly stated opposition to government censorship and spying. Enthusiastic popular rights adherents who cited Fukuzawa in support of their cause ignored, or did not know about, his acceptance of totalitarianism under certain circumstances. This was not unlike the government officials who overlooked his defense of liberal ideas. Clearly, Fukuzawa never supported the activities or the objectives of the **freedom and popular rights movement**. On the contrary, he approved of government actions designed to shut the movement down, a result that was essentially achieved by 1884 and totally secured with the Peace Preservation Law of 1887. On the other hand, Fukuzawa's writings were important to the arguments put forward by those in the movement and, consequently, a new audience was created for his published works. Also, as we will see later, he did support the establishment of a constitutional government that would include participation by at least some of the people in an election process to choose an assembly or parliament. It was the far-reaching demands of the more radical members of the movement for popular rights that Fukuzawa objected to.

The popular rights movement began with the ex-official Itagaki Taisuke's return to Tosa and his formation of a political party to agitate for a popular assembly. This theme was taken up by others with a variety of agendas that always included the establishment of some form of representative government. Through newspaper articles, pamphlets, and speeches in cities and villages, various disgruntled citizens of the Meiji state expressed their belief in the people's rights and their opposition to the oligarchy in control of the people's government. Ex-*samurai* who were penniless and unemployed, peasants struggling under the new taxation system, schoolteachers who had read Fukuzawa and other interpreters of Western "natural rights" theory, merchants and small-scale producers, and women all turned to the new political parties that sprang up to speak for everyone who had felt trampled upon by the government. A movement begun by ex-*samurai* was soon spread throughout Japan by elite rural leaders. Soon peasants sang songs about Itagaki's new **Liberal Party**, which, they believed, would usher in a more just world, a utopia.

Women followed the discussion of popular rights and sought a role in what they hoped would be an egalitarian society. They expanded on the ideas of equality that Fukuzawa and some his colleagues in the Meiji Six Society had timidly put forth in the *Meiji Six Journal*, drawing much broader conclusions from them. Freedom and equality would not just be a state achieved within marriage but would be realized between men and women in general. Two women, Fukuda Hideko and Kishida Toshiko, were particularly effective in their writings and speeches supporting the Liberal Party's platform for popular rights. They had extended the issue of women's rights well beyond what Fukuzawa and his colleagues had favored and anticipated full participation in politics with their male counterparts in the hoped-for new, democratic Japan. Kishida was especially eloquent in her demands for justice and civil rights for women. Her lectures were very popular, and audiences of both men and women packed the sites in the towns and villages she visited. Fukuda remembered how inspired she had been by Kishida's words. "Listening to her speech, delivered in that marvelous oratorical style, I was unable to suppress my resentment and indignation . . . and began immediately to organize women and their daughters . . . to take the initiative in explaining and advocating natural rights, liberty, and equality" (Sievers). Kishida was twenty years old at the height of her popularity in 1881, and the inspired Fukuda was sixteen.

Several of those who were leaders in the movement for freedom and popular rights had been students of Fukuzawa. Others had simply studied his works and interpreted his ideas more radically than he had intended. Professor Irokawa documented Fukuzawa's influence by recording instances of his books found in old storehouses in agricultural villages. Many schoolmasters in rural schools, it seemed, had used his texts. Irokawa cited the case of one ex-*samurai* who, as head teacher of a village school, would take his students to the seaside and require that they face the sea and recite a passage from Fukuzawa. Irokawa went on to list a number of leaders of the movement who had been educated by this schoolmaster. By 1879, however, Fukuzawa himself had denounced the popular rights movement, saying that its aggressive leaders had become destructive. He wrote: "They claim the people's rights for others, but do not know how to claim it for their own. . . . they then hate the government, want turbulence and, in the extreme case, resort to rioting. In sum it [should be called] *an anti-government party*" (Tamaki). On the other hand, Fukuzawa claimed at this same time to favor the establishment of a parliament, preferably along British lines, and he supported the government's promise of a constitution. He expected these political changes, however, to reflect careful discussion among intelligent and thoughtful government officials, rather than the rantings of mobs, as he characterized the participants in the movement for freedom and popular rights. The government certainly agreed with Fukuzawa, and from 1875 to 1887, issued more comprehensive censorship laws and made it illegal to assemble and speak out against the government. The criminalization of activities critical of the government crippled and then destroyed the popular rights movement.

Debates Over Constitutional Government

The Meiji oligarchy approached the political struggles of the 1870s primarily from two directions. On the one hand, they issued repressive laws and ordinances designed to stifle public discussion and enforced these through the establishment of an autocratic Home Minister and his central police force. In a more conciliatory manner, however, they also discussed the writing of a constitution that would include some sort of legislative assembly. They did, it seems, recognize the need to respond positively to public demands, which were causing so much strife. As one can imagine, the crucial question in the Council was how to write a constitution which would satisfy some of the demands of an angry public and still make sure that they, the oligarchs, retained control of the government. In the ensuing discussion, Iwakura and Itô represented those who looked to the example set by Otto von Bismarck in the imperial state of Germany created in 1871. This model provided for a constitution which sanctioned power in the hands of an emperor guided by a prime minister and appointed cabinet but with modest power given to an assembly elected by a select few. Yamagata also endorsed the German model but argued for a constitution with as few democratic rights as possible. His concern was not to mollify the Japanese public, but to find a compromise that would ensure continued oligarchy power while impressing the Western powers, who still held the upper hand in their treaty relationships with Japan. Ôkuma lobbied for a British-style parliamentary government with a popularly elected assembly made up of different political parties and a cabinet controlled by the party that held the majority in the parliament. Itagaki, ex-official and leader of the new Liberal Party, wanted to take the entire issue out of the hands of the ruling oligarchy. He pressed for a constitutional convention of the people to decide the form of the new government and set regulations for a popularly elected assembly.

Fukuzawa, too, was involved in the debates over constitutional government. He, of course, had observed firsthand and then written about the design and function of different constitutional governments in the United States and several nations in Europe. More importantly, he had translated several Western government studies and had presented his own version of the political history of civilization in general, as it might be applied to Japan. He, like others, wanted to apply his understanding of Western political theory to Japan in such a way that his nation could draw even with those in the West. While he did not agree with radical pronouncements and aggressive activities of the adherents of popular rights, he did believe that his study of the progress of Western civilization confirmed the necessity of a national assembly. He claimed in his 1899 autobiography that he had written a famous long article supporting establishment of an assembly that had been published as an anonymous editorial in a widely circulated newspaper. Although he said he had offered this treatise to the publishers in 1879 simply to amuse himself, it "was the immediate forerunner of the widespread discussion; so I think I am right in thinking that I set fire to the fuse that ignited the whole." While this statement, written with hindsight, exaggerates Fukuzawa's role in initiating constitutional discussion, there is no doubt that he did play a role in the debates on representative government.

Because Fukuzawa had access to Council members, he could express his opinions in less public arenas. Behind closed doors, and at the highest levels, he argued that the position held by Itô, Iwakura, and Yamagata was too autocratic. On the other hand, he approved of Ôkuma's plan, which centered on the British model and which achieved constitutional government in a more timely fashion. At the same time, Fukuzawa was averse to publicly signing his name to this opinion. Consequently, it was a *Keiô* graduate, influenced by Fukuzawa, who wrote the Ôkuma document, parts of which were published in Fukuzawa's journal. The oligarchs, who were opposed to Ôkuma's plan, were furious at Fukuzawa for exposing this idea in a public forum. One wrote that he was "arguing enthusiastically for radicalism," and called him a threat to the government in power (see Tamaki). Fukuzawa tried to mollify this individual by claiming, in a roundabout way, that the article in question could not be actually attributed to him. Just the same, the damage had been done, and when Ôkuma fell from power for different reasons, Fukuzawa found himself on the the Council's bad side as well. Not only was Ôkuma dismissed from the cabinet, all of his followers, many of whom were *Keiô* graduates, were fired from their government positions as well. Fukuzawa was furious, both with the government's action against Ôkuma and with himself for getting into this fractious situation. He determined once again to stay out of government service and distance himself from oligarchy debates.

With Ôkuma gone, Itô was free to lead the Council of State in the establishment of a constitution. The **Meiji Emperor** announced in 1881, as instructed by the Council, that he would present a constitution to the people and open an assembly by 1890. In 1882 Itô left for Europe to study the German model and other examples of constitutional government in earnest. Meanwhile, the radical Itagaki pressed his Liberal Party to continue its demand for popular rights and a freely elected parliament; Ôkuma, with the help of several Fukuzawa followers, established the moderate **Constitutional Reform Party**, calling for parliamentary government within the next four years; and a pro-government party called the **Constitutional Imperial Party** was formed but gained few adherents, as the government was not really interested in fostering the growth of political parties.

Fukuzawa, with the hindsight of almost twenty years and his anger at the government cooled, wrote in his autobiography that it was his agitation for parliamentary government in the late 1870s and early 1880s that pressed the oligarchy to promise a constitution and a national assembly by 1890.

Before the Constitution was actually promulgated by the emperor in 1889, the government passed new repressive laws, which ended the threat from the radical left, the Liberal Party, and the popular rights movement. After Itô left for Europe, Yamagata became head of the Council. He was the most autocratic of the oligarchs and took particular aim at the dreaded political parties. He tightened up loopholes in the press and assembly laws and issued new repressive decrees which gave the new Home Minister, Yamagata himself, and the prefectural governors additional powers to suppress activities deemed anti-government. In 1887, the government presented its first **Peace Preservation Ordinance**, which regulated the press, public meetings, and secret societies, as well as tightening censorship laws. Severe punishments were spelled out. It also gave the Home Minister, Yamagata at this time, the power to make any regulations appropriate "to prevent the distribution of political circulars" (Mitchell).

The new Meiji Constitution gave all power to the emperor, who was to be assisted by a cabinet appointed by him, with the advice of the oligarchs. It also provided for a two-house **Diet** [Parliament]. The upper house of the Diet was composed of nobles elected by each other and members of the imperial family appointed by the emperor. The lower house, essentially a debating society, was elected by men who paid a specified and high land tax. Women, who had worked hard within the Liberal Party for civil rights, were written out of the Constitution. To emphasize their inferior position, in 1890, just as the first Diet was about to be convened, the outgoing cabinet of the Council of State revised its ordinances on public meetings and political parties so as to deny women's participation in any political activities. They were prohibited from joining political parties or attending political meetings. This law remained in place until 1922, when women were finally allowed to participate in politics, short of voting or running for office. Women were not permitted to fully participate in political activities until after World War II in 1946.

The year 1890, then, saw the start of a new era of government, with an Imperial Constitution and an elected Diet. Yet national power still rested for the most part in the hands of the oligarchs. For example, for the next decade members of the oligarchy alternated in the prime minister's post, and the Home Ministry, controlled by an oligarch, continued its repression of the citizenry. However, Itô, Yamagata, Matsukata Masayoshi, and a few other powerful figures did have to continuously watch their backs, for the largest political party elected to the new Diet was the reconstituted Liberal Party.

Had the Constitution taken the form that Fukuzawa and his friend Ôkuma had favored, the Liberal Party's victory would have given them control over the Diet and the Cabinet. Under the so-called Meiji Constitution, however, the Meiji Emperor appointed the Cabinet. Of course, he made his appointments on the basis of the advice given him by his inner circle, the oligarchs. Fukuzawa was disappointed by this outcome. He believed the emperor should be above day-to-day politics and the running of the government. He saw the emperor as the catalyst for the people's allegiance to the nation and the embodiment of the national polity and in this he was in agreement with the new government.

Given the increasingly repressive censorship laws, Fukuzawa had to be careful in his writings about political and social issues. In 1882, he had begun publication of the *Jiji Shinpô*, a daily newspaper, in which he wrote a regular editorial column. In addition he continued to publish pamphlets and books, and to write for other journals. In all, he wrote on topics such as moral teaching, education, rights of women, and national policies. He had learned his lesson of not tangling with the government well, and many of his writings in the 1880s and 1890s were couched very carefully so as to avoid both the press laws and the personal hardship caused by inflaming someone in the government. He did not always succeed. Three times during the 1880s and once during the 1890s articles he wrote were censored, and his newspaper was banned for a week or more. However, since his own thinking had become more conservative on the issues that mattered to the government, during the last two decades of his life Fukuzawa did not often clash with the authorities.

VI

Social and Cultural Debates

Politics was not the only arena in which Fukuzawa debated during the last quarter of the nineteenth century. In fact, he was more absorbed by social and cultural matters. Issues relating to education and the rights of women led the list of prominent topics that he presented before the public. He found an eager audience for ideas on educational theory, and what he wrote and said became influential at the highest levels. He found a less engaged audience in the case of women's rights and far fewer colleagues to either contest his ideas or move his ideas further along, but he persisted; and his commentary on women was quoted by Japanese feminists long into the twentieth century. In these debates Fukuzawa had access to the public through his speeches, his books, and his newspaper, *Jiji Shinpô*, which he launched in 1882, and which continues today as the *Sankei Shimbun*.

Battles over Educational Theory and Practice

One primary reform that the oligarchy inaugurated in the early 1870s was the formation of a central Ministry of Education. This bureaucracy, in turn, issued the School System Law of 1872, known also as the Fundamental Code of Education. This complex nationwide plan for all levels of education primarily followed the French model but included borrowings from school systems in Germany, Holland, England, America, and Russia as well. On paper, the system provided for four years of compulsory coeducational primary schooling and then separate middle schools for boys and girls and higher school and university education for boys only. Students who went beyond elementary level had to pass rigorous entrance exams for admission to each new level of education. In addition, the plan provided for teacher training schools for men. The proclamation introducing the school system adhered very closely to Fukuzawa's ideas as expressed in the first pamphlet of *An Invitation to Learning*. The initial curriculum was heavily influenced by Western writings, especially Francis Wayland's *The Elements of Moral Science*, which Fukuzawa had translated and used extensively in his works, and by Samuel Smiles's *Self-Help*, the era's most popular Western book. In fact, the government assigned the translations of these two Western books and Fukuzawa's pamphlet as the first texts approved for the curriculum. Therefore, the Ministry of Education, in essence, declared itself committed to Western moral values, practical learning, and science as the basis of the nation's education of its children. The government had joined Fukuzawa in his call for "civilization and enlightenment."

Very early on, it became evident that establishing a universal system of education was going to be a struggle. It would not be as easy to bring educational uniformity and change nationwide as it had been for Fukuzawa to reform his small *Keiô Gijuku*, situated, as it was, on one small plot of private land in Tokyo. The Ministry of Education and the ruling Council of State would take fire immediately from several different directions. First, administrators at the many Tokugawa **terakoya**, or temple schools, which centered their curriculum on Confucian teachings and Japanese nativist thought, objected to the new school system on philosophical grounds. Other citizens objected to the complexity and foreignness of the curriculum. The texts used in the public schools, the same ones Fukuzawa used in his small school, were much more difficult for public elementary students than for the older students at *Keiô*. Indeed, these books were too complex for many of the teachers. So arguments over the new school system's curriculum and theory of education began immediately. These were not settled until 1890, when the Emperor Meiji issued his **Rescript on Educa-**

tion, which became the final word on moral education and patriotism.

Such issues of teaching methods and content were troublesome, but Japan's leaders believed they were solvable. More difficult were economic and social issues. There was little money available for bricks and mortar, teachers' salaries, and equipment, even for just the required four years of elementary schooling. The government was not able to pay for the system they had created and had to charge tuition. The economic shortfall worsened throughout the 1870s, hitting an especially bad point in 1877, when Saigô's Satsuma Rebellion consumed so much of the treasury. Many citizens, especially, but not exclusively, in rural areas, balked at paying fees to send their sons and daughters to study in schools the parents neither understood nor admired. Peasants complained that it was outrageous that they should pay to school a son and at the same time lose his labor in the field. Outrage grew to the point in many communities where groups of peasants and townspeople torched school buildings; kept their children, especially daughters and second and third sons, from attending schools as required; and generally rioted and caused destruction to underscore their opposition to the law. The disruptions and damage intensified as the movement for freedom and popular rights stirred up political and social confrontation in the late 1870s and early 1880s. During the twenty-year period following the Ministry of Education's initial announcement of four years of compulsory education for all children, school enrollment for boys only grew from 40 percent to 65 percent and for girls from 15 percent to 30 percent. During the same time, educational theory and school curricula were in continuous flux.

In 1879, a new education ordinance was issued, which changed the form and content of the system to reflect a more nationalistic perspective. School curriculum and expectations of students at all levels as well as teacher education reflected the commoners' wishes. School attendance was no longer mandatory, *terakoya* schools were used as public schools, foreign influences were muted or discarded, and moral teachings reflected more traditional thinking. Fukuzawa was alarmed and dismayed, for his text, along with the Smiles and Wayland books, was withdrawn from the curriculum as too Western. In the mid-

1880s, Mori Arinori was named Minister of Education. He instituted a German-style system, dominated by a curriculum that featured Japanese nationalism, with the result that compulsory, nationwide schooling was finally accepted by the public.

Mori, the Meiji Six Society founder, had spent several years in the West as a representative in Washington, D.C., and as Ambassador to Great Britain in the 1880s. He was well versed in Western thinking but believed that, while Western science was important to study, equally important was moral education based on Japanese ethical concepts such as consideration for others within the state and family. This suited the society of the late 1880s well, for it counteracted the attitudes of individualism and independence espoused by Western thinkers and Japanese writers like Fukuzawa. Such ideas by this time were considered selfish. The objective of schooling at the elementary level, under Mori's plan, would be to train the mind, the spirit, and the body toward success at work on the land and in the factory. In this way education would serve the government's goal of national progress. Higher-level education would be for a select few and so would be less constrained. Overall, education would allow for individual development, but its primary purpose would be advancement of the state; and it would, therefore, promote discipline, friendship, community support, and allegiance to the nation. Mori was assassinated in 1889, and his educational vision, which was considered too liberal by some, was altered to focus even more strongly on service to the emperor and nation. In 1890, the Emperor Meiji, encouraged by conservative thinkers such as the oligarch and military leader Yamagata Aritomo, issued the *Rescript on Education,* which established a neo-Confucian foundation for education and would continue to set the tone for schooling until after World War II.

Fukuzawa on Education

Fukuzawa spent much of his life involved with private education, and throughout that time he generously placed his thoughts before the public on both practical and theoretical educational issues. Fukuzawa's ideas on curriculum, educational theory, moral education, and other topics can be found in almost all of his primary publications. These would include his didactic editorials in his newspaper, *Jiji Shinpô*; his published plans for the structure and programs of *Keiô Gijuku*, which grew into *Keiô* University; and his philosophy of education as it was revealed in his own family interactions. In all of these practical manifestations of Fukuzawa's educational theory, he, unlike the Ministry of Education, never surrendered his allegiance to Western thinking and science. Nor did he falter in his support of private education. In fact, he took advantage of the chaos caused by the compulsory education law and the government's inability to fulfill its own requirements to open his own elementary schools in Nakatsu, Kyoto, Osaka, and other places as satellites to *Keiô Gijuku*. These schools, which exemplified his interest in educating young children as well as older students, prospered until the early 1880s, when the government schools became financially competitive. Also, in 1874, he inaugurated his own elementary school on the *Keiô Gijuku* campus, beginning a tradition of pre-collegiate education at *Keiô* that continues today. By the mid-1870s, then, Fukuzawa was firmly established as both a spokesman on education and as an educator himself.

The late 1870s and early 1880s were chaotic times for public and private schools. Even *Keiô Gijuku* suffered economic setbacks from the fallout of the Satsuma Rebellion of 1877. Enrollment decreased and tuition was inadequate to cover the school's expenses. Fukuzawa became very concerned, for he shouldered the primary expenses of the school, which were offset only slightly by the collection of tuition. He managed to survive this difficult economic time through contributions from successful *Keiô* graduates and supporters. From that time on Fukuzawa began to withdraw from absolute control and financial support of the school and worked with others to set up a foundation that would own and run the school. Fukuzawa's contribution would be the land and buildings, which he owned outright. In this way, Fukuzawa managed to move the college from near extinction in the late 1870s, to recognition as the first modern institution of higher learning in Japan by 1890.

Keiô Gijuku, however, did not exist in a vacuum. Fukuzawa found that his philosophy of education and the curriculum of his school put him in the line of fire during the education debates throughout the 1880s. The most heated exchange during this period involved the issues of moral education and a curriculum based on Western models. On both of these issues Fukuzawa was confronted by government officials. He had his supporters, however, most prominently Okuma Shigenobu, who in 1882 founded Tokyo Semmon Gakkô, which later became **Waseda University**, *Keiô* University's primary private school competitor even today. In spite of criticism from more conservative educators, both Fukuzawa and Okuma continued to follow a curriculum heavily influenced by Western thought, even as that choice became less and less acceptable in the public schools run by the Ministry of Education. Fukuzawa's school tended to emphasize economics and business, and Okuma's was more directed toward politics, but both were founded on independent thinking and practical learning rather than moral instruction. As Fukuzawa repeated over and over throughout the 1880s and 1890s, his students were simply expected to develop good character and act properly. They did not need specific courses in moral education to ensure that outcome.

More concretely, Fukuzawa debated the decade's turn toward an emphasis on moral instruction in editorials in his newspaper, *Jiji Shinpô*; in speeches at *Keiô*; and in public discussion. Because he seemed to be on the wrong side of the Ministry of Education, he was continuously defending himself against accusations that he was committed to Western philosophy, had forgotten his Confucian roots, and had failed to teach his students the social relationships appropriate for subjects of the emperor. Fukuzawa tried to write and talk his way out of the criticism by affirming his allegiance to the emperor and his patriotic support of national policy. But he also tried to suggest that the Meiji generation was different from those in the past and that education, even moral education, had to incorporate the changes that were inherent in the inevitable progress of this new civilization. He said in 1882, "I shall not reprove the endeavors of the present moralists for trying to apply the classical [Confucian] books in moral instruction, but I pray that the classical principles will be left to naturally adapt themselves to the contemporary trends of society and popular opinion . . ." Furthermore, given the new world Japan had entered, with its emphasis on international competition and foreign trade, he queried, "Will a doctrine of the Chou dynasty [Chinese Confucian era c. 600 B.C.]—when the best policy was to consolidate the center to the neglect of the outlying areas—apply to this world of turbulent vicissitudes?"(1883) And in 1885, he boldly stated, "Academic activities, when they remain aloof from human affairs, will only be mental exercises, and the researcher, too, will become a playboy of society. Those inept Confucianists belong to this type." In a speech to *Keiô* alumni in 1889, he proudly stated that education at his school included human and social studies and that it trained the student's mind to reason sufficiently to be able "to challenge the old Chinese philosophy which had been the pillar of our minds."

Fukuzawa carefully and respectfully debated the Ministry of Education throughout the decade of the 1880s, but there was no doubt that what he said challenged the evolving official educational standard. By 1890, however, all debate on education was halted by the promulgation by the emperor of the *Rescript on Education*. This brief document, drafted by officials with the aid of Yamagata Aritomo, became the framework for education until the end of World War II. It was put forward as his Imperial Majesty's own words; and a copy of this document, together with a picture of the Meiji Emperor, had a place of sacred honor in every school in the country. The *Rescript*, which contained the fundamental principles for all elementary education, was based on Confucian morality redefined by late nineteenth-century official doctrine, which embraced the sacredness of the emperor.

The people were admonished in the *Rescript* to maintain right relationships among themselves and to revere the emperor, whose lineage could be traced to the creator gods of Japan. Further, there was an expectation that all Japanese people would serve the emperor and his nation even, if necessary, unto death. The *Rescript* began, "Our Imperial Ancestors have founded Our Empire on a basis broad and everlasting and have deeply and firmly implanted virtue. . . ." This virtue was to be maintained through a national unity of emperor and subjects; filial piety toward parents; and right relationships between husbands and wives, brothers, sisters, and friends. It was to flower through an educational program that would "develop intellectual faculties and perfect moral powers," that would inculcate respect for the laws, that would nurture courageous service to the state, and that would support dutiful acceptance of the infallibility of the imperial way in generations past and for all generations to come. The debate about the purpose of education; allegiance to the emperor and the state; and that most important item in the curriculum, moral instruction, had effectively come to an end.

In the face of such educational conformity, however, *Keiô Gijuku* continued to follow Fukuzawa's often-repeated plan for educational instruction that would encourage independent, creative thinking. As Fukuzawa said in 1893, "*Keiô Gijuku* is a school of learning, but the objective of our members is not confined to the study and analysis of books. We attach great importance to their personal independence, that of their households, and of the nation." (1893) Yes, patriotism to the nation was important, but this would best be effected through individuals and their households gaining independence. And by independence he implied economic independence through professional success. Such economic success on the individual and national level would bring respect in the international community and equality with the powerful Western states. Fukuzawa was proud to repeat again and again that, while *Keiô* was interested in scientific and technological training, it had also included human (cultural) and social studies in the curriculum, and this included the study of the history and economics of the West. In conjunction with this, he insisted that the students learn English, which he suggested would help them to gain practical employment even if nothing else did.

Exemplifying his continued deference to the Western scholarly tradition, Fukuzawa persuaded three American professors, two graduates of Harvard and one of Brown University, to assume chairs in the arts, economics, and law, thus providing a new luster to his faculty. He also hired several noted Japanese scholars. The prestigious faculty, together with generous donations, including a large one from the Imperial Household, and a new educational plan, brought about the launching of *Keiô* University in 1890. Fukuzawa's school, based on his educational theory, had matured over three decades into an institution that could compete with the new Imperial University in Tokyo.

四女 滝　　五女 光
三女 俊　　次女 房　　　長女 里

Fukuzawa's daughters, mid-1880s. Left to right: Shûn, Taki, Fusa, Mitsu, Sato (Courtesy of Fukuzawa Memorial Museum in Nakatsu.)

The Education of Fukuzawa's Children

In 1883, Fukuzawa's wife, Okin, age thirty-eight, gave birth to their ninth and last child. Fukuzawa himself was forty-eight at this time. The two older sons, Ichitarô and Sutejirô were now twenty and eighteen respectively. The five daughters were Sato, age fifteen; Fusa, age thirteen; Shûn, age ten; Taki, age seven; and Mitsu; age four. A third son, Sanpachi, was two years old; and the last son, Daishirô, was born in 1883. This completed the family. All children were healthy, and Okin, who had given birth nine times in twenty years, was healthy, too.

As can be imagined, the education of his children was very important to Fukuzawa. He had begun his own formal education somewhat late, and he valued that approach for his own children as well. According to Fukuzawa's remembrances late in life, his older sons and daughters were invited to play and enjoy themselves far more than most children and were only expected to take up the rigors of schooling as they grew older. Even then, Fukuzawa, who sent his two sons to Tokyo schools, found himself dismayed by the discipline and demands placed upon them and soon withdrew them from that environment. The answer, he decided, was to send these boys to *Keiô*, where they would experience a Western-style education, plenty of physical exercise, and a comfortable environment. In 1883, the two older sons were ready for higher education; and Fukuzawa, a rich man by this time, sent both of them to Oberlin College in Ohio for beginning college studies and English language practice. Following this introduction to American higher education, he sent the eldest, Ichitarô, to Ithaca, New York, to study at Cornell University, where he received a degree in English literature, and the second son, Sutejirô, to Cambridge, Massachusetts, where he graduated in civil engineering from MIT. Later, Fukuzawa sent his third son, Sanpachi, to the University of Glasgow in Scotland, from which he graduated in mathematics in 1904; and his fourth son, Daishirô, who entered college after his father's death, remained in Tokyo, graduating from *Keiô* University. In addition, in 1874, Fukuzawa sent his only nephew, who was like another son, to London to study. This description makes clear that Fukuzawa held higher education, most particularly in Britain and the United States, in very high regard; believed that his sons and nephew would benefit from the experiences abroad as well as the study; and was wealthy enough to finance the tuition, living costs, and subsequent foreign travel for five young men.

What is missing from this educational picture? None of the five daughters was given the opportunity for higher education. As elementary students the older daughters were placed in *Keiô* school for a while, but soon returned home, where all five daughters received their schooling. Fukuzawa congratulated himself in his 1899 autobiography for the freedom that he allowed all of his children and the fact that he and his wife treated them all equally. "Among my nine children, we make no distinction at all in affection and position between boys and girls." He was very proud of the fact that all five of his daughters had married successfully. This outcome, a good marriage, as he would point out in 1899, in his *"New Greater Learning for Women,"* was the ideal for all young women. Beyond their good health and the finding of husbands, he had little else to say about his daughters' lives or their education.

The Cambridge University Fukuzawa scholar Carmen Blacker, however, had the opportunity to interview the fourth daughter, Taki, in Tokyo in the early 1960s. Taki had married Shidachi Tetsujirô when she was eighteen, slightly older than her mother was when she married Yûkichi. Professor Blacker stated in a footnote to her 1964 book on Fukuzawa that "I (Blacker) was disappointed to learn from Mrs. Shidachi that Fukuzawa failed entirely to put his precepts into practice in the upbringing of his own daughters. He left their education entirely to their mother, who was 'very conservative' and convinced of the innate inferiority of women." Blacker went on to say that Taki told her that she was "never allowed out alone, never allowed to express her opinion in the presence of her elders, and never allowed to speak to guests when they came to the house." Except for the fact that she learned English, her education was much like that of other girls, probably, in fact, quite close, including home schooling, to that of most *samurai* daughters under the Tokugawa *bakufu*. And, by the age of eighteen, she was married off without any opportunity to express her own opinion on the match.

Fukuzawa, rather than his wife, bears greatest responsibility for the conservative, traditional education of his daughters. Given his pontificating on the equality among his own children and his many writings, as we shall see, on the rights of women, it is difficult to understand how he managed to overlook the inferior position in which he placed his own daughters. Although he was opposed to the radical political movements of the late 1870s and early 1880s, he had to be impressed by the similarity in what young politically active women were saying about the education of girls to his own early theories of education. Kishida Toshiko was quoted in an 1883 newspaper as saying "Daughters must be taught basic economics and the skills that would permit them to manage on their own. Even a woman who expects to be protected during her husband's lifetime must be able to manage on her own, armed with the necessary skills, if he should die." (Sievers) This sounds so similar to Fukuzawa's pleas for individual independence and his emphasis on economics in the educational curriculum. It is not as if there were no schools for girls. Missionaries had opened Western-style schools, Fukuda Hideko opened a school for boys and girls, and there were the public schools. If these did not appeal to Fukuzawa for either political or other reasons, after educating the daughters at home, he could have considered sending one or more of them for higher education to Japan Women's University, which his friend Ôkuma Shigenobu had helped to found. This lapse in Fukuzawa's thinking is truly puzzling. On the other hand, we have a small window on Fukuzawa's thinking in a published letter in which he urged his compatriots not to send their daughters to Western schools, where a non-utilitarian program might make them less desirable marriage candidates (Huffman, 2003).

Fukuzawa on Women's Rights

Fukuzawa and others in the Meiji Six Society wrote articles in the mid-1870s in favor of equality between husbands and wives within marriage. He and Mori Arinori were particularly emphatic on this issue, and Fukuzawa officially witnessed the marriage contract professing equality between Mori and his bride, Tsuneko, which solemnized their well-publicized Western wedding in 1875. Less ballyhoo surrounded Mori's divorce in 1886, also accompanied by a written contract signed by both parties. Mori's second marriage, which took place in June 1887 to the youngest daughter of Iwakura Tomomi, leader of the 1871 Iwakura Mission to the West, followed Japanese traditional custom. This marriage of less than two years was cut short by Mori's assassination in 1889. No one offered any reason for the earlier divorce, but it was speculated that the first wife had had an affair with someone in England while Mori was ambassador there. At any rate, the contract proclaiming equality within marriage did not make Mori's home life secure. Fukuzawa was completely content with his marriage to Okin. Neither she nor he had a wandering eye, and Fukuzawa considered that both he and his wife were equal at home and within the family. It was, perhaps, this experience of contentment that led Fukuzawa to discuss publicly the inferior position of wives in Japanese society.

It took Fukuzawa about a decade to follow up on his early commentaries on women's rights in *Encouragement of Learning*, *Outline of the Theory of Civilization*, and the *Meiji Six Journal*. But after Fukuzawa settled into his role as newspaper editor and began writing his regular editorial column, he returned to his earlier crusade to expose and decry the inferior position of women in Japan and to make suggestions for improving women's lives. His comments on women, begun in 1885, were segmented to fit the short format of editorial writing and thus appeared over several consecutive issues. In these essays Fukuzawa took up such issues as the psychological and emotional devastation caused to wives by husbands who acquired concubines or mistresses, the physical illnesses wives experienced due to inadequate sexual fulfillment, the inequality of wives caused by the laws governing household registration, the financial disadvantage all women experienced because they could not own property in their own name, the unfairness of granting more opportunity and love to male children over females in a family, and the necessary evil of *geisha* and prostitutes. Unlike other writings, in these opinions Fukuzawa was not responding directly to the writings of others. He was simply trying to highlight issues about which he had been concerned for many years, with the hope social changes might result.

Perhaps Fukuzawa's most vociferous commentary concerned what he considered the licentious practices of upper-class men, especially government officials, and the effect their behavior had on their wives. Here he was undoubtedly directing his words at Matsukata Masayoshi, Finance Minister during the early 1880s and later Prime Minister, and Itô Hirobumi, who became Prime Minister for his first term in 1885. Both of these men were well known for their concubines and, in Itô's case, for his flaunting patronage of *geisha*. Fukuzawa approached this subject of male misbehavior from several different viewpoints. First of all, he believed the attitudes and activities of philandering husbands were indefensible on moral grounds. Beyond that, he felt that such behavior was detrimental to the family. In some cases children born to concubines did not even know who their real mothers were, and often children were raised by legal wives who were not sympathetic to the concubine's child. Thus the family, which, Fukuzawa believed, constituted the foundation of the nation, was compromised. Furthermore, he believed that wives suffered physically and emotionally from inadequate sexual gratification because of the wayward ways of their husbands. A wife suffers from "nervous diseases, hysteria, or uterine disorders" due to "lack of satisfaction in her sex life," Fukuzawa wrote. On the other hand, he sadly pointed out that prostitution, which he called an evil institution, was a necessity for single men, especially those who were too poor to ever marry. As immoral and degraded as the prostitute might be, she was a necessary evil in society; in fact, she could be called a martyr for social stability. Because "a man is human when he is dressed properly in clothing, but when naked, he is a beast," it is necessary "to depend on prostitutes to maintain safety and order in society," he concluded.

Some of the ideas that Fukuzawa presented in his editorials were quite radical for the era. He believed, for example, that a primary reason for women's inequality was financial. Women had difficulty making an adequate living independent of male family members. Moreover, upper-class women seldom had jobs outside the home, and they were not permitted to own property in their own name. Consequently, even women of wealthy families could find themselves penniless and dependent on the goodwill of first their fathers and then their husbands. He suggested, "There should be a law passed providing that no land or house can be owned except in women's names, and also that no public loan bonds can be sold or bought except in women's names. This would be a very effective device." He was certain that if women held a monopoly on real estate their position in the society would "improve a hundredfold." He looked forward to the promised revisions in the Civil Law, for he expected that the legislators would give consideration to this issue of property ownership. In 1898, with the passage of the **Meiji Civil Law**, he would find that the *samurai* practice of inheritance by the eldest son would be codified, and his idea of provision of property for women would be firmly rejected. In 1899, in his autobiography, Fukuzawa commented that, although his eldest son was his primary inheritor according to this law, he had provided for his wife at an earlier date.

Fukuzawa made another bold suggestion to bring equality to a marriage. He noted that it was the family register, and not any ceremony, that legalized a marriage; determined the status of each member of a family; and announced the family to which each member of society legally belonged. A woman was not considered married until her name was written into her husband's family register. Sometimes this did not take place until after she had given birth to a child. Until her name was registered, she had no status in that family. Also, a woman was not allowed to remain in her birth family's register unless her husband was being adopted into the wife's family. Fukuzawa suggested that at the time of marriage the husband and wife combine parts of their names to form a new name and use this new name to establish an independent family with a separate register. This, he believed, would symbolize the equality that should exist in the marriage.

Fukuzawa wrote often about the importance of the education of girls for the advancement of the family as well as the nation. He suggested that creating an atmosphere which would make it possible for girls to grow and prosper was very easy. In the beginning a baby girl should simply be loved as much as a baby boy. Throughout childhood parents should see to their daughter's development of both mind and body. "In her schooling and other education never discriminate because of her sex. Give her freedom to meet people and make friends, and let her learn about society and world as much as about household affairs." Give her an equal share of the family property and let her manage it herself, he suggested. From such treatment a daughter would "be able to go through life without depending on a man and the spirit of independence [would] naturally be born in her." And so Fukuzawa presented his ideal for equality within the family. He even followed this ideal with his own family up to a point. He raised five daughters whom he loved very much, as much as his sons, so he claimed; and he appeared to give them educational advantages, though through home schooling, in their early years. He could have continued to test his theories as his daughters grew. Instead, just like most of his contemporaries, he considered their upbringing successful because each daughter entered into an early and prosperous marriage to become a dependent wife. As he stated in an editorial in 1899, "When a woman reaches maturity . . . she should marry."

In 1899, toward the end of his life, Fukuzawa wrote once again in *Jiji Shinpô* about women. At this time he gave what he called "random" talks on men and women and on society. He also wrote two more focused commentaries on *The Greater Learning for Women* by Kaibara Ekken, a seventeenth-century thinker, whose description of proper female behavior was seen as the model for upper-class women of the late nineteenth century. These collected essays, *A Critique of the Greater Learning for Women* and *The New Greater Learning for Women*, represented, in the first case, Fukuzawa's debunking of the ancient scholar's life prescriptions for women and in the second, Fukuzawa's own revision of those rules. It had been over ten years since Fukuzawa had addressed women's rights publicly, and his change of tone was quite obvious. There is none of the radical talk about women's ownership of property or even the simply liberal attitudes toward education. Fukuzawa had become more conservative and more in tune with the *Rescript on Education* and the new Family Civil Law, making just an uncontroversial nod or two toward equal rights for women within the family.

In both essays Fukuzawa spoke primarily to women in the new upper classes; and consequently what he had to say had little application to the majority of women in the society, that is, peasant women or the large number of women working in textile factories. For example, there is much said about the treatment of servants and household management in general, where Fukuzawa praised the abilities of women but placed their accomplishments within the home. He commented that although few women could "understand and discuss the politics and economics of the country," and, in fact, appeared to be "ignorant of these matters," if one changed "the subject to daily household business—from food, clothing, and the management of servants, social intercourse and the exchange of presents, entertainment of guests, recreation for different seasons to the education of children, the care of invalids, and all the problems of a household," then women would prove to have "intellect, precision, and subtlety, beyond description." When he spoke once again about women's education, he argued for the need to educate a woman for her role in the household so that she might "be called an accomplished lady." And further, "The economics and law which women should study are not at the level that bankers and lawyers master. I am recommending that they study these subjects as a personal accomplishment for the same reason that women of *samurai* households of bygone days carried daggers in their bosoms. For women, knowledge should be regarded as a personal accomplishment which may turn useful in self-defense." During the late nineteenth century there were men, though very few, who defined equality for women to include political rights and believed that women could function as well as men outside the home. Fukuzawa was not one of these radical thinkers.

Since these articles were written in 1899, they followed the passage of the 1898 Civil Law, which was to rule family life in Japan until after World War II. Interestingly, Fukuzawa referred to particular sections of this new civil law with apparent agreement and a nod to its forward-looking character. Since much of this law was based on *samurai* custom, this acquiescence on Fukuzawa's part is both surprising and not surprising. Fukuzawa had been critical of the *samurai* status laws of his childhood, and he considered himself a defender of equality of the sexes. One would, therefore, surmise that the new family law, which gave ultimate power to the household head and the eldest son, would not fit his thinking. But then, although Fukuzawa spoke out against the hierarchies of Confucian thought, he had never completely abandoned his early Confucian schooling. His adoration of things Western did not mean that he had surrendered entirely to Western traditions. He retained a Confucian streak in spite of all his adulation of the West. In the case of women, it is clear that had every wrong that Fukuzawa exposed been righted, women would still not have had equality with men in their homes or in the nation. He did not, as we have seen, place much value in higher education for women, nor did he approve of political rights for women; and he did not really believe that most women were capable of moving beyond responsibilities in the home to those in the society as a whole. Just the same, for his time, he was more outspoken and more concerned about women's rights than the vast majority of men in Japan.

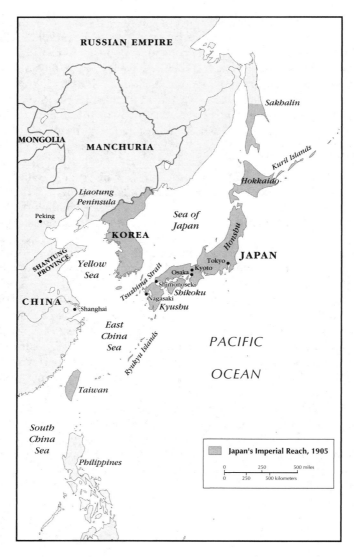

Japan's Imperial Reach, 1905.

VII

"Rich Nation—Strong Army"

Ever since the "Treaty of Amity and Commerce Between the United States and Japan" was signed in 1858, followed soon after by similar treaties with European nations, Japan had felt the sting of her inferior position in the international community. These treaties gave foreigners the right to set tariffs for Japan and to employ their foreign legal systems on Japanese soil. There wasn't a moment after 1858 that Japanese officials did not think about throwing off the yoke of these unequal treaties. Beginning in 1869, with the issuance of new ordinances by the Meiji oligarchy in the name of the Meiji Emperor, renegotiation of these treaties with foreigners was always the driving force behind institutional reforms. The Iwakura Mission, which went to Europe and America in 1871, had as its primary mission discussions with American and European officials toward the goal of abolishing these treaties, which so favored the West. This aspect of the trip was a total failure. There would be no quick and easy renegotiation of extraterritoriality laws or the commercial treaties. The Japanese discovered that they would have to prove themselves the West's equal before the foreigners would take them seriously enough to grant Japan international parity.

Over the next two decades every Japanese official who studied or traveled in the West sought knowledge and practical understanding that would improve Japan's standing among the ranks of nations so that she would be accepted on equal terms.

The slogan *fukoku kyôhei*, rich country/strong army, which Fukuzawa had first used in one of his publications, became the leadership's shorthand for its efforts to raise Japan's status in the world. All of the political and intellectual elite, regardless of their specific ideologies, believed that Japan had to increase its wealth through industrial and agricultural development, and its military strength through advanced training and modernized armaments, in order to show the nations of the West that Japan was their equal. Consequently, when Itô Hirobumi went abroad in the early 1880s to study constitutional government, he was not just looking for the best political system for Japan. He was looking for a political system that would be recognized by Western governments as enlightened and therefore appropriate for a world player. When Yamagata formulated the rules and regulations for the new conscript army, he looked to examples from the West with an eye toward impressing the Western over-lords. When the oligarchs invested government money in new enterprises, they anticipated both individual and national wealth that would eventually swing the nation's balance of trade in Japan's favor. Developing a rich country and a strong army, it was hoped, would finally bring about the repeal of the unequal treaties and raise Japan's status in the world.

Fukuzawa was in full agreement with the ruling oligarchy on the issue of the nation's military and economic status. In his last two decades he grew more and more to appreciate the necessity of strong banking and commerce and, in general, the growth of national wealth through capital accumulation as the primary underpinning of national power. He also backed the raising of a strong military. He commented that he had gained more insight from observing the practical course of Western military intrusion than from all his theoretical reading about national rights and responsibilities. His comment in his *Outline of a Theory of Civilization* that "international diplomacy is really based on the art of deception" marked the beginning of his support for an aggressive foreign policy. Through the 1880s and 1890s he would become more and more influential as he wrote and spoke ceaselessly of the need to draw equal to the West in foreign military daring backed by industrial power. Behind the scenes he would pull the strings necessary to bring about the financial success that would back the government's foreign adventures. Finally, he would help to mold a public attitude of nationalism that would support Japan's ventures in imperialism.

Industrial Development

The Meiji government's first decade was a bumpy one. The oligarchy had so many new institutions to create for the twin purposes of establishing domestic tranquility and impressing their foreign overlords. Laws were promulgated which established local governments, a national bureaucracy, a national banking system, an international trade system, a central police force, a national conscript army, a compulsory education system, and so forth. Next, they had to ensure adequate tax collection to run the new bureaucracies and help finance industrialization, while at the same time leave enough private capital available to encourage business and commerce. The hope was that eventually Japan's new business and industry would be able to compete with the industrialized West. This was a huge task, and in those first few years, and during the first fifteen years, it looked as if the oligarchs were not going to be successful. By the late 1870s Japan's finances were in such disarray that economic failure seemed imminent. At this point, in 1881, the Council of State made a dramatic personnel change toward reorganization of the government's financial operations. This gamble paid off.

The Satsuma-Chôshu members of the council ganged up on Finance Minister Ôkuma Shigenobu, ex-*samurai* from Hizen and Fukuzawa's close friend, and threw him out of the government. Among other things, this meant Ôkuma's plan to solve Japan's economic crisis by seeking foreign loans was repudiated. The council then turned to Matsukata Masayoshi, a lower-level *samurai* from the Satsuma clan, for their new Minister of Finance. Matsukata's mandate was to put Japan's economic system on a stable footing. The actions he took over the next few years were draconian, as he squeezed every bit of surplus out of the peasants through high taxes, deflated the economy, and accumulated a surplus in the national treasury. Matsukata was well aware of the pain his policies caused the poor majority of the country, but he was convinced that this was necessary if Japan were to stabilize economically. He sought and gained the assurance of both the emperor and the leading oligarchs that they would back his policies, even to the point of using military force in the event of public rioting. Matsukata stood firm, the government backed him, and over the next four years he cut government spending, sold government-owned projects and industrial plants to private citizens at very low rates, instituted a central banking system, raised taxes, depressed the prices of rice and other commodities, and thus turned Japan's finances around. At the same time many, many people suffered impoverishment and there were indeed riots, which were suppressed by the new conscript army.

The new policies based Japan's economy on the capital surplus squeezed from agricultural production. This capital was destined for investment in industries, which would be primarily in the hands of private entrepreneurs, who often received direct government handouts or benefited from cheaply sold government-owned capital equipment. One of the primary industries Matsukata determined to foster was that of textile production. Here was an export-based industry that could bring hard currency into the country. Moreover it was an industry that cost relatively little to run either in capital expenditure or in labor. Most of the workers were farm women and young girls who were paid little, and the building and equipment costs for this labor intensive industry were relatively small. Matsukata stated early on that Japan's economic future depended on the growth of the textile industry to the point that it could compete with Western exports.

Of course, other more capital-intensive, heavy industries also emerged, such as shipbuilding, mining, railroads, machine and tool manufacture, and heavy military equipment. In these enterprises we see the formation of family businesses and *zaibatsu* conglomerates, which would dominate Japan's industrial sector for decades to come. Names such as Mitsui, Mitsubishi, Yasuda, and Sumitomo would dominate the business landscape until the end of World War II and would even, in some cases, rise again after the war. Agriculture, the sector of the economy primarily responsible for payment of taxes, also improved its production through technological advancement. Unfortunately, however, the farmers did not see much of the wealth that the new "rich country" was amassing. For them another slogan, **kuni no tame ni**, "for the sake of the country" described their sacrificial role in producing a "rich country and strong army."

Fukuzawa: The Entrepreneur

A primary theme in Fukuzawa Yûkichi's private life and public pronouncements was his belief in the importance of individual effort and independent action. He said over and over in his books and his speeches that education should provide practical knowledge and rational thinking and that a student should strive for independence for himself and for his family. If those goals were achieved, the natural outcome would be independence and success for the nation as well. He firmly supported the policy of building a wealthy country based on entrepreneurial skill, as well as building a powerful military, which could guarantee Japan's independence. Though he had spent several decades lauding the West, by the early 1880s he was at least as concerned with achieving parity with the West through flexing economic and military muscle. He still believed it necessary to study Western ways, and his *Keiô Gijuku* was a model for the importance of assimilating Western thinking; but as a great patriot, he wanted Japan to rise to the level of achievement of other industrialized nations.

One satisfying corollary to his thinking was his belief that achievement of national wealth would come about through the efforts of entrepreneurial individuals who, in the process, would also become wealthy. Fukuzawa counted himself within this group. He was helped in his own efforts to obtain wealth by the fact that he knew the primary government players in Japan's development, like Matsukata and Itô. He also counted many of the new industrial leaders among his friends and associates. Furthermore, the success of the graduates of his school made him "father" to many business leaders of the future. As his own wealth grew, he began to underwrite important economic ventures, especially in the financial world. And, through his close contacts with successful leaders, many of whom had been associated with *Keiô*, he became a kingmaker in Japan's business world. There was very little going on in Japan's business world that Fukuzawa was not aware of, and when he wanted the public to know about any of it, he wrote about it in his influential newspaper, *Jiji Shinpô*.

Fukuzawa had already begun his entry into the business world when he discovered he could realize greater royalties from his writings if he published his books as well. In 1869, he bought up a large supply of paper on speculation, employed artisans, and began to publish his own books. This was a rudimentary operation, but it gave him a taste for this particular business. That same year one of Fukuzawa's *Keiô* students established a trading company, in which Fukuzawa soon invested and which became known as Maruzen. It was established along the lines of a joint stock company, the first in Japan, as studied by Fukuzawa in his research and observation of British business practices. The first Maruzen, which provided Western books, stationery, clothing, and pharmaceuticals, was opened in Yokohama, but by the beginning of the 1870s, a branch was established in Tokyo. This was followed shortly by branches in Osaka, Kyoto, and Nagoya. Although Fukuzawa did not run the operation, he was undoubtedly the primary force behind its business plan, a major investor, and a business consultant. He also guided the Western book division and advised the translation division, which, at his request, published translated versions of Montesquieu, Mill, and Spencer, among others. Fukuzawa's own publication of 1873, *Bookkeeping,* became a primary reference work for this and other new companies; and *Keiô* graduates, uniquely qualified by the school's business division, joined Maruzen management through Fukuzawa's recommendations. According to Professor Tamaki, an authority on Fukuzawa's business accomplishments, "Although Fukuzawa did not sit on the board of directors, he was effectively the strongest man in the management [of the company]." Maruzen continues today as a major company, which is also a primary importer of foreign and translated books.

In the mid-1870s Fukuzawa backed the establishment of a commercial school run by an American who had been brought to Japan by Mori Arinori. Fukuzawa was particularly drawn to this project because he believed that Japan must take control of foreign trade, which was at that time in the hands of Westerners. A school of commerce, he thought, would be an important weapon in what he considered to be a commercial war between Japan and its foreign overlords. Although he studied and translated Western books on business and management and he was happy to engage Western teachers of these subjects, he was quite angry with the stranglehold that Western merchants had over the treaty ports. He believed that once Japanese commercial traders secured the right to deal directly with the great centers of wholesaling in the major cities of the world, Japanese importers would increase in stature and wealth. It was, he concluded, the greedy middlemen in the foreign enclaves, who maintained their advantage through the unequal commercial treaties, that mortgaged the future of locally owned trading companies.

Foreign monopolies, unequal commercial treaties, and lack of native business skills were not the only barriers Fukuzawa overcame on his road to entrepreneurial success. Like the government, Fukuzawa's own business ventures experienced a huge financial setback from the economic fallout of Saigô Takamori's Satsuma Rebellion. We have seen that this led to Matsukata's 1881 monetary deflation, accompanied by hard times for many citizens. Fukuzawa also experienced financial difficulties as a result of the rebellion. His solution was to protect his investments by going into banking. He began in 1879 by subscribing to the Maruya Bank, a savings bank, formed by associates of Maruzen to protect their business capital. This gave Fukuzawa the idea, which he shared with then Finance Minister Okuma, for a specie bank. Fukuzawa believed in free trade. He saw development of an expanded export market as vital to the future wealth and independence of the nation. Consequently, he saw the need for a bank that would protect specie, that is, gold and silver. He reasoned that the payment of gold and silver to foreign importers for their goods meant a major loss of treasure from Japan to foreign merchants. The unequal treaties stipulated that import duties could not be set by the Japanese government, and the rates of currency exchange were set arbitrarily in favor of foreign money. The result was that much hard wealth, that is, valuable silver and gold coins and gold bars, or specie, was leaving the country to fill the coffers of foreign businessmen with inflated profit. In 1880, Fukuzawa secured financial contributions in return for ownership shares for the establishment of a specie bank. This money came from leaders of the Yasuda, Mitsubishi, Sumitomo, and Mitsui companies, as well as other businesses and organizations. Thus Fukuzawa's idea was realized in the Specie Bank of Yokohama. Over the next few years, with the help of the new Finance Minister, Matsukata, foreign branches of this bank were set up, and the Specie Bank's smooth operation paved the way for Matsukata's central bank, the Bank of Japan.

In the 1880s and 1890s, Fukuzawa invested in other businesses; trained students to become businessmen; recommended his own students for significant positions; and advised and contributed to successes in mining, insurance, banking, and other enterprises. He worked with the leaders of Mitsui, Mitsubishi, and other well-known companies who were gathering the lion's share of Japan's growing industrial wealth. In this he did well for his country and perhaps even better for himself. He also spread the wealth of *Keiô* knowledge throughout the business world, where individual graduates formed a sort of management clique of experience and success. Perhaps one of his greatest successes in "paternalism" was the career of his own nephew, Nakamigawa Hikojirô. Returning from his studies in London in the late 1870s, he first took up employment in government service, then became editor of Fukuzawa's newspaper, next president of a railway company, and finally director of the Mitsui Bank. In this last position he is credited with leading that bank to greater wealth through shrewd investment in business and industry and acquisition of textile companies during the government's bargain sales of the 1890s. He was indeed a credit to his uncle, who had educated him and financed his advancement. Like so many others, he was also a significant link in Fukuzawa's long chain of influential affiliates.

Fukuzawa: The Journalist

In the first issue of *Jiji Shinpô*, March 1882, Fukuzawa claimed that his would be a "free and independent" newspaper. By this he meant that it would not be tied to any particular political party. In his first editorial in the first issue he pointed out that while Japan had a government, many political parties, various businesses and industries, and many scholarly associations, his newspaper, in the spirit of independence, would not show favoritism toward any of these groups, but would try to be of assistance to all of them. "Our primary aim in taking the name *Jiji* will be to record development in recent civilization, to discuss goals and events related to the progress of that civilization, to keep abreast of each day's new currents, and to report them to the world." He further stated that the newspaper would "render judgments solely on the basis of whether something helps or hurts the nation." (Huffman, 1997) He referred to the characters *jiji* in the newspaper's name because this newly coined word represented a compound of the characters for recent civilization and method of progress. The *Jiji Shinpô* was to provide all sorts of news about the advancement of civilization and the methods by which this progress was to be obtained. Here Fukuzawa carried forward the themes that he had been pressing in his writing, speeches, and school for over two decades.

Professor James Huffman has pointed out that this daily newspaper was innovative in that it intended to provide a balance between news and opinion and, though it would most certainly discuss political matters, it would not be beholden to any particular ideology. Huffman goes on to say that from the first, *Jiji Shinpô* covered foreign news as well as local and national news, editorial comment, and stories of daily living, or in other words, wrote about all aspects of the manner in which modern developments were "civilizing" people's lives. As in other areas of Fukuzawa's entrepreneurship, he intended that this venture into journalism should make a profit. To this purpose, within the first year he began to include advertising in the newspaper. This ran the gamut from services, such as insurance and shipping, to products like books, telephone poles, cosmetics, tobacco, and wine. Ads were often placed prominently on the front page. In 1886 Fukuzawa began to use the first page exclusively for advertising and that same year opened an advertising agency. The combination of advertising, increased circulation, and Fukuzawa's management skills assured increasing profitability for the enterprise. Huffman concludes that Fukuzawa's overall success "held tremendous importance for the future of journalism" in Japan.

Like his school, Fukuzawa's newspaper focused on information that would be useful to businessmen. All of his writings had stressed practical education toward the goal of independent individuals, independent families, and an independent nation. These same goals were to be emphasized in *Jiji Shinpô*. While he wrote about political events, such as the promulgation of the new constitution and elections for seats in the Lower House of the Diet, more space was given to commercial news. His newspaper listed data on stocks and prices in the rice markets, export figures for the textile industry, banking news, and anything that would be useful to businessmen and industrial leaders. Consequently, he attracted the educated reader, who was willing to pay the higher price that *Jiji Shinpô* cost. The careful attention paid to economics, industry, and business, both at home and abroad, also benefited from the college educated staff. Since two of the primary divisions at *Keiô* were business and journalism, it is not surprising that Fukuzawa hired many of his own graduates as reporters. Their background also meant that he could rely on them to write their own stories, a new idea in newspaper publishing of this time. *Keiô* was also a source of educated journalists for other newspapers, most particularly the one founded by Ôkuma Shigenobu in support of his Constitutional Reform Party. Every time a *Keiô* graduate joined a newspaper, a commercial firm, or a bank, honor and respect accrued to Fukuzawa; and this was often followed by influence and sometimes by financial profit.

As in the case of Fukuzawa's writings about women's rights, he used his editorials to express his own opinions and press for debate and action on any number of current topics. During the 1890s these included commentaries on government educational policy. In 1892, he began an editorial with the confrontational sentence, "The government has committed many blunders since 1881, and those in its educational policy are among the most serious ones." Fukuzawa was not timid when he felt he had an important wrong to right. He went on to say that such errors were not easily wiped away like a stain on a mirror; rather, they were more like opium, which penetrates the body so deeply that even when one stopped taking this substance the effects would linger on for months or even years. He then went on to state that while he was quite in favor of instilling "loyalty, filial piety, and patriotism" in citizens, the anti-foreignism and extreme intolerance that followed the incidents of 1881 manifested a trend that could disrupt society. By directing this criticism at events of a decade earlier and not mentioning the *Rescript on Education,* Fukuzawa was able to call for educational policy change without raising cries of disloyalty. On the other hand, he made it perfectly clear that he believed the policies implemented in the previous decade were responsible for the failures in education during the 1890s.

In the late 1890s, Fukuzawa used his editorial influence to criticize the spate of regulations that established central control for the choice and publication of elementary school textbooks. These laws, which encompassed private schools like *Keiô* as well as public schools, had been growing in number and strength since 1885. After the promulgation of the constitution and the establishment of the Diet, the **House of Peers**, the upper house, passed appropriations for funds to support national expenditures for textbooks. Fukuzawa was furious and wrote in 1897 that national control over instructional materials meant that "people below the ordinary officials" were responsible for both writing and choosing texts and that "whenever an inspector, from personal prejudice," opposed a text "the book is rejected without the least hesitation." He went on to exclaim that the "choice of textbooks should all be left free to each school, with the Ministry of Education limiting its activity to an inspection to prevent truly objectionable books from being adopted." Fukuzawa, as usual, included a few words of compromise within his firmly anti-government stance. There is no doubt that Fukuzawa recognized that his successful newspaper business could be a tool of national influence as well as a provider of personal wealth.

Fukuzawa: The Imperialist

Like many government officials and other influential leaders, Fukuzawa saw the unequal treaties as the mark of Japan's inferior position within the international community. As a patriot and strong supporter of the emperor, Fukuzawa often editorialized about Japan's need to stand up to the West. The corollary to this position in his mind was the need to build an army capable of backing a policy of national independence. Of course, it went without saying that Japan could not and would not instigate war with any Western nation. How, then, could she show her strength and leadership? In Asia, of course. Fukuzawa had agreed with the oligarch's decision not to follow Saigô Takamori's plan of sending an expedition to force Korea's hand in the early 1870s. However, by the late 1870s and early 1880s Fukuzawa saw promise in establishing a hegemony over Korea under the guise of helping Korean reformists civilize their backward country.

At this time Fukuzawa concluded that the prime motivator of Western foreign policy was the use of power, and he believed that Japan should aspire to the same approach. He stated in 1878 that he rejected his earlier belief in natural reason as the basis for foreign relations. Negotiated treaties based on rational discussion, he had determined, might be "high-sounding" but were of little value in the real world as described by Charles Darwin and Herbert Spencer. Nations gained advantage on the basis of power and strength and the axiom "survival of the fittest" applied to nations as well as species. As Fukuzawa exclaimed, "A few cannons are worth more than a hundred volumes of international law. A case of ammunition is of more use than innumerable treaties of friendship. . . . There are only two ways in international relations: to destroy, or to be destroyed." (Hwang) And the next year, 1879, he added, "A nation does not come out on top because it is in the right. It is right because it has come out on top." (Blacker)

In his first issue of *Jiji Shinpô* in 1882, he directed his new thinking specifically toward Korea. This would be a case he would make over and over throughout the decade. He argued that, while Japan was advancing on the road to civilization, Korea was still a backward country. This was of great concern to Japan because of Korea's proximity. Japan's neighbor's inability to civilize or defend itself meant that the stronger nation would have to help Korea in the same way that America and Europe had helped Japan in the past. In other words, Japan needed to both civilize Korea by teaching it modern ways and protect Korea by sending the military to assure Korea's independence. He did not want to see Korea either remain under the protectorate of backward China or fall into the hands of Western overlords such as Russia. Consequently, in the early 1880s, Fukuzawa became involved with a Korean reformer, Kim Ok-kyun, who hoped to overthrow the Korean monarchy and establish a Westernized political and economic system, which would follow Japan's leadership. Kim had been inspired by Fukuzawa's writings. Furthermore, during his stays in Japan, he had been guided directly by his Japanese mentor. It might even have been Fukuzawa's influence that gained Kim a loan for his movement from the Yokohama Species Bank. In any case, Fukuzawa definitely supported Kim, whom he saw as the leader to bring Korea out of the dark ages. After Kim's 1884 attempted coup failed, he fled to Japan, becoming an embarrassment for the Japanese government, most especially the several high officials who, along with Fukuzawa, had helped in his scheme.

In March 1885, Fukuzawa, believing there was little hope anymore of civilizing either Korea or China, published his famous essay "On Leaving Asia" in *Jiji Shinpô*. The title represented Fukuzawa's conclusion that Japan's neighbors were never going to grow out of their backward Confucian past. Consequently, it was time to show the West that Japan's more advanced thinking and scientific accomplishments set her apart from the other nations in her "neighborhood." He explained, "It is not different from the case of a righteous man living in a neighborhood of a town known for foolishness, lawlessness, atrocity, and heartlessness." This righteous man's actions (Japan's) could not be compared with the "ugliness of his neighbor's activities" (China and Korea). Given the confusion that might arise from the proximity of these three nations, he continued, "It is better for us to leave the ranks of Asian nations and cast our lot with civilized nations of the West." Furthermore, having now joined the West, Japan should treat its unenlightened neighbors in the same manner that the Western powers had treated Japan. Over the next ten years Fukuzawa would reiterate that both China, a nation he had criticized for most of his life, and Korea, a nation he had wanted to help, should be treated in whatever manner was necessary for the maintenance of Japan's own independence and her acquisition of international equality.

In the fall of 1885, another group of Japanese, led by Liberal Party official Oi Kentarô, developed a new plot to overthrow the Korean monarchy. Their intention was to establish a "liberal" government sympathetic to the people's rights. This group was stopped by the authorities in Nagasaki before they could board a waiting ship for Korea. Among the members jailed was Oi's mistress, Fukuda Hideko, who had been one of the prominent women in the freedom and popular rights movement. Unlike Fukuzawa, whose activities on behalf of Kim did not even meet with disapproval, these radicals were all thrown in jail. They remained locked up until 1889, when they were released under a general amnesty called for at the time of the promulgation of the new constitution. As in the case of Fukuzawa, the apparent dissonance between liberal attitudes toward internal politics and harsh imperialist power politics toward a foreign country was in accord with late nineteenth-century Western thinking, which saw no contradiction between one form of political thinking at home and another abroad.

Fukuzawa was not alone in his analysis of Japan's relations with her Asian neighbors. His attitude predated the official government policy of the 1890s, but anticipated its perspective. When the conservative military leader Yamagata Aritomo addressed the Diet in 1890 as Prime Minister, he expressed his fears that Russia or Britain might move into Korea and that such action would threaten Japan's sovereignty. Therefore, he proposed a foreign policy that would set both a "line of sovereignty" and a "line of advantage" in an effort to protect Japan. Although these were different boundaries, both would have to be protected militarily. In the first instance, he included all of the territory currently occupied by Japan. For the second, he extended that line to include nearby lands that were close enough to potentially cause harm to Japan. This immediately included Korea, and, as time went on, it would include parts of China as well.

At the same time, Itô Hirobumi, who held the position of prime minister several times, coined the phrase "peacetime warfare." By this he meant that continuous rivalry for trade expansion and investment opportunities by all of the industrialized Western countries should be considered a kind of warfare. This "peacetime warfare" as realized in East Asia was an operation that Japan should become involved in. Under this policy, Itô and others saw opportunities in Asia for investment in railroads, industry, and mining. Japan needed to compete with the successful Western nations who were carving up the world for their political and commercial advantage. Much had already been accomplished at home to impress upon the powerful Western nations that Japan was politically and economically mature. Now it needed to show that it was militarily and internationally powerful as well. The scene was set, the argument made, for Japan's entry onto the world military stage by way of protecting Korean "independence." Simultaneously, negotiations for eliminating the unequal treaties, thus assuring Japan's political acceptance into the international arena and her economic freedom to set tariffs, were finally moving toward a successful conclusion.

The Sino-Japanese War (1894-1895)

On July 16, 1894, Japan and Britain signed a tariff agreement that would, over the next five years, eliminate the extraterratoriality laws that had deprived Japan of her sovereignty. Tariff autonomy and rights of British citizens to live anywhere in Japan were also a part of the new relationship. Just two weeks later, on August 1, Japan declared war against China. Two

Top: Hooray for the Great Japanese Empire; Right: Hooray for the Emperor and Empress; Left: Hooray for the Navy and Army. (From *Jiji Shinpô*, January 1, 1895, p. 2)

events had moved the Japanese to military action. First, Kim Ok-kyun was murdered in exile in China and his corpse sent back to Korea. There, Korean officials defiled the body by dismembering it as an example to all who might oppose the monarchy. Japanese newspapers, led by Fukuzawa's *Jiji Shinpô*, expressed their anger. In May, Fukuzawa demanded, through an editorial, that the Diet vote "no-confidence" in Prime Minister Itô's cabinet because of its lack of immediate military action. This did not happen, but Fukuzawa's point was made. Secondly, a religious group attempted an uprising; and the Korean monarch asked for China, Korea's traditional protector, to intervene. Chinese troops headed for Korea in June. Again the newspapers clamored for action. By late July the government could vacillate no longer. The outcry in the press had rallied the people. Japan sent troops to fight the Chinese army saying that China's intrusion into the Korean Peninsula had broken a diplomatic agreement between the two nations. China had promised, said the Japanese government, to inform them before any move into Korea. China refused to back down, and Japan declared war.

This was a popular war in Japan. And Japan's newspapers made it so. It was assumed that Japan's forces were stronger than China's and that a successful war would assure Japan's hegemony over Korea, her superiority over China, and her acceptance as a full-fledged military power by the West. Japan achieved victory upon victory, and each one was well publicized and cheered unanimously in the Japanese press and then by the public. Fukuzawa and his newspaper were perhaps the most jingoistic of all. Fukuzawa himself declared this to be a "religious war" and patriotically offered more than once to donate a huge sum of money for the war effort. His newspaper, like others, published extra upon extra, often within the same day, feeding the public's excitement over the progress of the war. People clamored for all the news they could get about battles, conditions for the troops, responses of military families, and so forth. Newspapers sent war corespondents to the front who followed the troops, suffering the same trials of difficult terrain, bad food, and unsanitary conditions, and consequently providing a firsthand experience of war for the public at home. At every juncture Fukuzawa and his newspaper were there to wave the flag and urge the government and the army on for the glory of Japan. *Jiji Shinpô* was eagerly read, and circulation soared. Everyone in Japan was made to understand that Japan's successful debut on the world military stage would mean equality with the West.

In the end Japan suffered only a relatively small loss of life and treasure, and the whole country was exhilarated when China was forced to come to Shimonoseki in April 1895 to sign a peace treaty. The final terms of the peace treaty were very favorable to Japan. There was independence for Korea, which would in practice mean a Japanese protectorate there. Japan received treaty ports, commercial rights, and navigation rights within China and a huge indemnity to be paid in gold. Perhaps the jewel, however, was the new territories ceded to Japan: Taiwan, the Pescadores, and the Liaotung Peninsula in China. (The Peninsula would have to be surrendered later as a now-fearful West, in the form of Russia, France, and Germany, pressured its new rival to give this prize up.) Japan now had an empire and was recognized by all as the superior nation in Asia. Military strength and patriotism fed by newspapers meant a new, powerful Japan had emerged in the 1890s. Fukuzawa was involved at every moment and unabashedly saluted the success of Japan's new stage of "civilization and enlightenment" gained through the acquisition of wealth and military strength. Two years after the war, in 1897, all of the Western nations had renegotiated the unequal treaties. Japan was a power to be reckoned with.

Thus throughout the 1890s, Fukuzawa's influence through his school; his relationship with the financial world; and, most particularly, his newspaper was so strong that members of government sought to win him to their side. From the late 1880s until 1898, Fukuzawa's friend Ôkuma, once again a powerful figure, was tapped for service in three cabinets, thus giving Fukuzawa special entrée to the government. In that same period the prime ministership had alternated between Yamagata, Matsukata, Itô, and Ôkuma, all leaders with whom Fukuzawa had enjoyed private discussions. When Matsukata followed wartime Prime Minister Itô in 1896, he consulted with Fukuzawa. As a result of the indemnity from the Sino-Japanese war, the treasury had received a large influx of gold, and Matsukata determined that Japan, like some European countries, should use this "windfall" to go on the gold standard. That is, he intended to peg the currency of Japan to the international price of gold, a policy he could effect because the currency would be backed by actual gold in vaults. This would give Japan's currency greater stability, and the nation would gain even more respect abroad. Fukuzawa, initially opposed to this action, could have troubled the government with a newspaper campaign against the proposed policy. Matsukata, believing that it was important to bring this journalist, who had influence in the economic world, around to his way of thinking, sought Fukuzawa's support. The personal effort Matsukata employed secured Fukuzawa's endorsement, thus guaranteeing favorable editorials from *Jiji Shinpô* on this issue.

By the end of the century Fukuzawa had successfully used his understanding of Western capitalism for profitable gain for himself and his family and used his influence as educator, newspaper editor, and entrepreneurial kingmaker to place students and associates in significant roles in the business and financial worlds. Like most leaders of his era, he had also turned his Western learning from the goal of "civilization and enlightenment" to a nationalism that would support Western-style imperialism against Japan's neighbors. He saw Japan's growing military strength as a counterweight to the West's territorial and economic aggrandizement within Asia and campaigned in his newspaper to abandon a policy of trying to "civilize" an independent Korea or China. Instead, he believed, Japan should respond to the "backwardness" of these "neighbors" in the same superior manner the West had treated Asia, including Japan, in earlier decades. Japan must become a leader in Asia by acting with appropriate strength and power for the benefit of the "neighborhood." Fukuzawa's jingoistic journalism was seconded by the other newspaper editors, but his association with those in official power made his opinion more influential. He had reconfigured his liberal thinking, acquired from studying Western thinking, into a kind of nationalism that could compete with the West in military and financial power. In the process Fukuzawa and most other influential leaders accepted oppression of other nations and acquisition of territory as a necessary and, in fact, a positive step on the road to national progress and development. The fittest and strongest would survive, and, through the leadership of the more powerful, the weaker would eventually become civilized. Fukuzawa and his nation had become imperialist.

Epilogue: Fukuzawa's Legacy

Fukuzawa walking on *Keiô* campus next to debating hall. *Keiô* student on left, Fukuzawa's caretaker on right, 1900. (Used with permission of the Fukuzawa Memorial Center at *Keiô* University.)

By the turn of the twentieth century, Fukuzawa Yûkichi had withdrawn from leadership of all of his enterprises. In 1890 he delivered a speech inaugurating the rebirth of *Keiô Gijuku* as *Keiô* University and celebrating the new departments headed by Americans. He also introduced the new president, who would be responsible for management of the school. During the rest of the decade, Fukuzawa, although he had withdrawn from active participation in *Keiô's* administration, still followed the operations of the university with great interest and continued to work toward achieving its financial stability. At the unveiling of his statue on the university grounds in 1893, he restated his intention to leave the property occupied by *Keiô* and owned outright by himself to the university. He suggested this could be considered the "school's first endowments." At his sixtieth birthday celebration, which occurred a year late, in 1895, due to the Sino-Japanese War, he rehearsed the part he had played in *Keiô's* rise to fame. Once again, he admonished those present to "establish your personal independence and that of your households" and to work for the benefit of the nation as a whole. In much more than just an afterthought, he urged those present to "launch a new enterprise." In his 1896 speech to a small group of *Keiô* alumni and colleagues, he anticipated the end of his life and grieved for those older and younger who had already passed away. He concluded, "I shall never be satisfied to leave *Keiô Gijuku* a mere institution of learning; I aspire to make it the springhead of noble character and a model of intellect and virtue for the whole nation."

That same year, 1896, Fukuzawa resigned as editor of *Jiji Shinpô* in favor of his second son, Sutejirô. After graduating from MIT in Civil Engineering in 1888, Sutejirô had returned to Japan to work for a railway company. Later he joined his father at *Jiji Shinpô*, and in 1896, he took over as president of the company and editor of the newspaper. Yûkichi continued to write editorials until late 1898, but it was his son who made the business decisions and saw to increased circulation and continued profitability after the excitement over the Sino-Japanese War had ended. He followed his father's practice of running expensive advertising and focusing on commercial news of interest to wealthy businessmen, rich farmers, landowners, and affluent merchants. The newspaper continued to be the nation's most expensive, but it was one of the most successful, though its circulation was not in the top ten after the turn of the century.

Throughout the 1890s, Fukuzawa continued to be influential in political and business circles, especially during and immediately after the Sino-Japanese War. His support of the government's aggressive imperialist foreign policy was well known to the public through his newspaper editorials and to officials through private communication with important government officials. Fukuzawa's second son, Sutejirô, had married a daughter of Hayashi Tadasu. In 1871, Hayashi had been a translator with the Iwakura Mission, and when he left London, he was given books by a *Keiô* student destined for Fukuzawa. Hayashi moved up through government ranks, and in the 1890s, he became ambassador to China and then the primary negotiator of the peace treaty that ended the Sino-Japanese War. Afterward, Hayashi served first as Japan's ambassador to Britain and later as Foreign Minister in the cabinet. Here was an important friend who was also tied to Fukuzawa's family.

Fukuzawa had many close associates among the powerful. He conversed with prime ministers as well as lower officials. He sent many *Keiô* graduates out into the worlds of commerce, banking, insurance, textiles, and other areas of business and industry essential to Japan's economic development. His motto for *Keiô* students, "Learn and Earn: Earn and Learn" was taken to heart by many young men. At the end of the century Fukuzawa was famous throughout the nation among people of all walks of life, and his influential hand had guided many future leaders. Fukuzawa's legacy was already legendary.

In September 1898, Fukuzawa suffered his first stroke. Although this did not totally incapacitate him, it did leave him disabled. It was after this event that he dictated his autobiography. Perhaps his condition explains in part why the autobiography strays from reality. It appears written to support a uniformity of thinking throughout his lifetime, for it tweaks life experiences to present the man Fukuzawa believed he had always been. Although the autobiography is useful for outlining the notable events in his life, it is less accurate in plotting the twists and turns of his thinking.

In 1900, a famous Moral Code for *Keiô* students was presented as Fukuzawa's final essay. Indeed, this twenty-nine-point code followed his primary axioms, as revealed over four decades, throughout his educational career. It was, however, written by his eldest son, Ichitarô, and a few students. Beginning with a nod to the Imperial House, which "has reigned throughout the ages" the code promoted personal dignity, self-respect, independence, education, health and exercise, equality of men and women, sanctity of marriage, and the individual's duty as a citizen to serve in the army. It further stated that both men and women must support the nation even to the point of sacrificing their own lives. Fukuzawa's Moral Code, as it was known, was translated into English and became a text at *Keiô* University for both character building and the study of English. When someone suggested after World War II that it again become the Moral Code of *Keiô*, the opposition pointed out the militaristic and imperialistic features. It was not reinstated.

Fukuzawa suffered a second stroke on January 25, 1901, and he died on February 3. The funeral was held on February 8, and it is said that mourners came in the thousands, and the funeral procession stretched for miles. The **Lower House** of the Diet passed a resolution stating, "We recognize with great respect and admiration the profound contribution Fukuzawa Yūkichi made to Japanese education and to Japan." This was the first time the Diet had officially commemorated the death of someone who was not a member of that body. At the time of his death, he was sixty-six, his wife, was fifty-five, and all nine children were still living. His wife lived on until 1924, dying at the age of seventy-nine.

Fukuzawa's legacy *Jiji Shinpô* was carried on by his son Sute-jirô. Several family members continued his work at *Keiô* University. Fukuzawa Ichitarô, the eldest son, became chancellor of *Keiô* University after teaching there for several years. The third son, Sanpachi, was studying mathematics at Glasgow University in Scotland when his father died. Later he continued his studies at Leipzig University, returning home from Europe in 1907 to take a position as professor at *Keiô*. Shûn, Fukuzawa's third daughter, married Kiyooka Kuninosuke, and their son, Eichi, was sent by his parents at the age of seventeen to the United States to attend Cornell University, from which he graduated in literature. While in America, he bought a Model T Ford and a Kodak movie camera and drove across country in 1928, filming all the way. He returned to Japan to teach at *Keiô*. Later he translated his grandfather's autobiography and several other collections of his writings into English. The younger son of Fukuzawa's daughter Mitsu became an administrator at *Keiô* just after World War II, a fitting memorial to his mother, who died young.

Fukuzawa's youngest son, Daishirô, became a businessman. Perhaps, since his father had died before Daishirô was old enough to attend university, he did not have an opportunity to enroll in an elite institution abroad like his brothers. He remained at home and completed his undergraduate education at *Keiô* in the department of politics. Afterward, however, he went to America and studied at Harvard College before he became the executive director of Kawaragu Gas Company.

In contrast with his liberal writings on women, Fukuzawa wanted to see his daughters settled in traditional marriages. Consequently, he actively sought successful, educated husbands for his non-working daughters. The marriages he arranged would highlight the nuclear family with fathers accumulating wealth and mothers remaining at home to care for children and supervise large household staffs. It was his hope that the daughters would be as happy as he and Okin had been and that the husbands would not have a wandering eye. All five of his daughters married in accordance with their father's definition of an ideal marriage. Although all of them had been well educated, primarily at home; had studied English; and were cultured and artistically accomplished, none had been permitted to go on to higher education. Each one married by the time she was twenty.

The eldest, San, known as Sato, married Nakamura Teikichi, a chemistry teacher at *Keiô*, when she was just sixteen. Unfortunately, her husband died of tuberculosis when he was twenty-eight, leaving her with two young sons. Fukuzawa could not help but lavish favor on these, his first grandchildren, and he happily assumed responsibility for them and their widowed mother.

The second daughter, Fusa, also married a man connected with *Keiô*. He was a handsome student at the school who had caught Fukuzawa's eye. Iwasaki Momosuke had come to *Keiô* in 1883 at the age of fifteen, thanks to sacrifices made by his rural relatives, who were of modest means. Fukuzawa apparently saw great potential in this student, and so the conscientious father sought him as a husband for Fusa. The marriage proposal, as laid out by Fukuzawa, required that Momosuke assume the Fukuzawa name through adoption. In return he, a second son with no prospects of wealth through his own family, would become a son to Fukuzawa, with all the rights accruing from that status. In addition, as he had for his other sons, Fukuzawa would send Momosuke to America to travel, observe, and study in the West. Momosuke agreed to the arrangement and went to America's east coast from 1888 to 1890, returning to Tokyo to marry Fusa, then twenty. The couple had two sons in the next two years. Fukuzawa was right about Momosuke's prospects, for he distinguished himself over the years as a successful engineer, a clever entrepreneur, and a wealthy businessman. He became known as "the king of electric power" for dams he constructed to electrify the Kiso Valley, and one of his bridges in the area is still referred to as the Momosuke Bridge. He and his elder son founded a chemical company together in 1934.

Unfortunately, Fukuzawa's clairvoyance for Fusa's successful future in marriage did not extend to her happiness. Before Momosuke contracted his marriage, he had fallen in love with a *geisha* whom he could not forget. This young woman, Yakko, later Madame Sadayakko, was famous in the *geisha* community for her first lover, the Prime Minister, Itô Hirobumi. Fukuzawa had publicly criticized Itô for his style of life, which included many concubines and mistresses, and might have thought twice about the marriage arrangement for his daughter had he known about the connection between her intended and Itô's mistress. Momosuke, however, proved himself a proper gentleman by leaving his *geisha* lover at the time he married Fusa. Unfortunately, unable to live without Sadayakko, twenty years later, after she had ended her career as a famous actress, he openly left his wife and took Sada as his mistress. Since Momosuke was so wealthy, he was able to provide for his wife, his two sons, and his mistress in style. He built mansions for each of them, three for the legal family on his estate in the Shibuya area of Tokyo and one for Sada in Nagoya, near his electrical power business in the Kiso Valley. He, of course, lived with Sada in her "Futuba

Palace," near Nagoya Castle. In 1933, Momosuke, with Sada's blessing, returned to his wife, living his remaining five years on his estate in Shibuya, Tokyo. He died in 1938, while Fusa, out-living him by seventeen more years, died in 1955. According to her descendents, she never forgave Momosuke for the way he had treated her. (See Downer)

Fukuzawa chose another *Keiô* student for his third daughter, Shûn. Kyooka Kuninosuke entered *Keiô* as a young pupil in 1884, did a stint as an exchange student in England, and then returned to join a shipping company and to marry Shûn. Their son, Eiichi, spent considerable time in America and became his grandfather's primary translator into English. Shûn had con-verted to Christianity at seventeen, and though this made her rather strict with her children socially, it also inspired her to ed-ucate her daughter at the Sacred Heart School in Tokyo, quite a liberating choice for a Fukuzawa woman.

For his fourth daughter's husband, Fukuzawa actually looked for a suitable prospect outside *Keiô*, though not outside the world of business and finance. Taki, who complained to Carmen Blacker that her father never let her act independently, followed his wishes and in 1895, at the age of nineteen, married Shidachi Tetsujirô, a Tokyo Imperial University graduate, who had become a banker. He later entered the management ranks of Sumitomo Bank, an institution that at that time was run by a *Keiô* graduate. Taki followed her father's wishes as proper wife and mother to four daughters, but she wanted a career for her-self. To fulfill this desire, she founded a branch of the YWCA in Tokyo and managed it for almost thirty years. She died in 1970 at the age of ninety-four. Had she been permitted to follow her brothers' educational path, there is no doubt she would have achieved at least as much as they had, and perhaps more.

In 1897, at the age of eighteen, Fukuzawa's youngest daugh-ter, Mitsu, married Ushioda Dengorô, an engineer with a Mitsui manufacturing company. Fukuzawa, still deciding the fate of his daughters' marriages, was especially pleased with this arrangement as the chosen husband was the son of the noted moral reformer, Ushiodo Chieko. She was a member of the Tokyo Women's Reform Society, which had been organized in the 1890s by Yajima Kajiko, just after passage of the 1889 law preventing women from joining political organizations. The organization spoke out against social practices such as concubinage, prostitution, and drinking, all opposed publicly by Fukuzawa as moral ills. Mitsu and her husband produced two sons and a daughter before she died in 1908 at the young age of twenty-eight.

Since all of his daughters and his two oldest sons had married before Fukuzawa's death, he was surrounded in his final years by many grandchildren, whom he loved dearly. Included in this group as well were the children of his siblings, whom he had brought into the family, and many offspring related to *Keiô* school. There are any number of photographs that show him with his grandchildren and other schoolchildren as he walked about his property and the school grounds in kimono, carrying a walking stick. The kimono, he believed, was a much more sensible attire than Western clothes, and, one might add, it was easier to manage for someone as uninterested in maintaining his appearance as Fukuzawa was.

All Japanese have heard of Fukuzawa, and most revere him as a primary figure in Japanese history. What they actually know about his thinking or his contributions to Japan's nineteenth-century development is far from clear. He has unquestionably become an icon of liberal education and intellectual accomplishment, though it is doubtful that many Japanese could put these proclaimed attributes in detailed perspective. His face is seen by the Japanese every day, for in 1984, when the currency was changed and different faces were put on the bank notes, Fukuzawa's photo was placed on the ten-thousand-yen note, the largest bill. In 2004 most of the bills will once again sport a new picture; only Fukuzawa's 10,000-yen bill will remain the same. Given the economic recession that has embraced Japan for over a decade now, everyone uses this largest of Japan's currency notes every day. They need just look at their money for a second any day of the week to see the famous Fukuzawa. At the time the decision was made to put Fukuzawa's photo on this bill, only a few protested this choice. Those few naysayers believed that Fukuzawa had proved himself to be a chauvinist during his lifetime and would therefore represent Japan's reprehensible militarist and imperialist past. Most people, if they heard of this muted debate at all, did not know what it was about, for the nationalistic aspect of Fukuzawa's thinking had been forgotten in the aftermath of World War II. The history of Imperial Japan is not a strong subject in today's classroom, and so Fukuzawa's legacy tends to be reflected in the continued success of *Keiô* University, rather than his support of nineteenth-century imperialist adventures.

Fukuzawa's other continuing triumph was *Jiji Shinpô*, which had supported the Sino-Japanese War and, after Fukuzawa's death, the Russo-Japanese War of 1904-05. Under Sutejirô it also became famous, briefly, for its beauty contests and for its Go (similar to chess) columns. Few people today realize that the current *Sankei Shimbun*, with the third largest newspaper circulation in the nation, grew out of Fukuzawa's *Jiji Shinpô*. Fukuzawa's other entrepreneurial successes were achieved within financial and business groups and consequently are more difficult to trace. Professor Tamaki has done a great service to point these out in his discussion of Fukuzawa's commercial and financial contributions and to uncover the numerous *Keiô* students and industrial magnates who carried his entrepreneurial achievements forward. His legacy, though more difficult to highlight, lives on in banking, commerce, and insurance.

While Fukuzawa continues to be proclaimed by some to be a great philosopher, and his most famous works such as *Invitation to Learning* and *Outline of Civilization* are still in print in Japan, the public seldom looks carefully at the twists and turns of Fukuzawa's thinking over the years. He is more a hero of the past, or an idol, than a real historical actor. Often Japanese historians have not been particularly helpful in sorting out Fukuzawa's place either, for some tend to either praise his scholarship and his early "systematic" thought uncritically or damn him as an arch-conservative and thus ignore him. As we have seen, he was both liberal and conservative, both nationalist and individualist, both moralistic and materialistic, and all shades in between these polar opposites. Most definitely, however, he was a major figure in the second half of Japan's fast-changing nineteenth century, and as such his involvement with the crafting of the new Imperial Japan deserves to be studied.

Professor Tetsuo Najita of the University of Chicago has described Fukuzawa's thinking, and, in fact, his actions as "materialistic liberalism." He has further commented that Fukuzawa was not an idealist, as we might think after reading some of his works written in the 1870s, but rather a pragmatist who followed both the utilitarianism of seventeenth-century Japan and that of nineteenth-century Britain. He believed in the "rational pursuit of self-interest" and concluded that if an individual worked hard for what he wanted most, his achievements, combined with those of his neighbors, would push the entire country upward toward progress. Najita sums up his analysis thus: "An enormously successful pundit, critic, and educator, Fukuzawa played a pivotal role in the formulation and diffusion of an entrepreneurial ethic for modern Japan. . . ." By placing Fukuzawa's interests and accomplishments in a broader framework, Najita has avoided the temptation to get bogged down in either praise or damnation of particular actions. Fukuzawa, through his writing and his activities, helped to determine the shape of nineteenth-century Japanese history. Like so many significant players at that time, his thoughts and actions, especially toward the end of the century, included promotion of both individual and national aggrandizement. He praised the accumulation of wealth and power by a talented few like himself and wealth and power for Japan within the pantheon of power-seeking, imperialist nations. Both the individual and the national perspective that Fukuzawa proclaimed characterized late nineteenth-century thinking in both the Far East and the West.

A Note on the Sources

Many books on nineteenth-century Japan make reference to Fukuzawa Yûkichi, but there have been only two biographies written in English. In 1964 Carmen Blacker of Cambridge University wrote the classic *The Japanese Enlightenment: A Study of the Writings of Fukuzawa Yûkichi* (Cambridge University Press). She also translated Fukuzawa's "Kyûhanjô" ("Conditions in an Old Feudal Clan," 1877) which appeared in *Monumenta Nipponica* in 1953. It has taken almost forty years for a new biography to appear. *Yukichi Fukuzawa 1835-1901: The Spirit of Enterprise in Modern Japan*, by Norio Tamaki, a *Keiô* University professor, was published by Palgrave in 2001. Both these biographies are indispensable to a study of Fukuzawa. The Blacker work is dedicated to Fukuzawa's thinking and writing as interpreted through 1960s historical research methods. The Tamaki book is based on Fukuzawa's extensive collected works, including translations and newspaper editorials, and his letters. This work breaks new ground in its discussion of Fukuzawa the entrepreneur.

We are fortunate to have translations of several of Fukuzawa's writings into English, primarily thanks to the work of Fukuzawa's grandson, Eiichi Kiyooka, beginning with *The Autobiography of Yukichi Fukuzawa*, which was revised in 1972 (Shocken Books). He also translated *Fukuzawa Yûkichi on Education* (University of Tokyo Press, 1985) and *Fukuzawa*

Yūkichi on Japanese Women (University of Tokyo Press, 1988). Finally, in Japan Kiyooka has published three works specifically devoted to Fukuzawa's relationship with *Keiō* University. There is a complete translation of *An Encouragement of Learning* by David A. Dilworth and Umeyo Hirano (Sophia University Press, 1969) and Dilworth and G. Cameron Hurst translated *An Outline of a Theory of Civilization* (Sophia University Press, 1973).

Five general works of Japanese history that are invaluable are: *A Modern History of Japan* by James McClain (W.W. Norton, 2002); *A Modern History of Japan* by Andrew Gordon (Oxford University Press, 2003); *Premodern Japan* (Westview Press, 1991) and *Modern Japan* (Westview Press, 1986) both by Mikiso Hane; and *Early Modern Japan* by Conrad Totman (University of California Press, 1993).

Other sources that have been particularly useful for this study will now be listed under the chapters for which they were most helpful. The authors of specific translations and/or quotations are mentioned in the text.

General Background for Tokugawa Japan—Harold Bolitho, "The Tempō Crisis" in *The Cambridge History of Japan, Vol. 5*, ed., Marius B. Jansen (Cambridge University Press, 1989); Harold Bolitho, "The Han" *in The Cambridge History of Japan, Vol. 4*, ed. John Whitney Hall (Cambridge University Press, 1991); Harold Bolitho, *Treasures Among Men, the Fudai Daimyo in Tokugawa Japan* (Yale University Press, 1974); John Whitney Hall, "The Bakuhan System" in *The Cambridge History of Japan, Vol. 4*, ed. John Whitney Hall, (Cambridge University Press, 1991); Tetsuo Najita, "Oshio Heihachirō" in *Personality in Japanese History*, ed. Albert M.Craig and Donald H. Shively (University of California Press, 1970); Kozo Yamamura, *A Study of Samurai Income and Entrepreneurship: Quantitative Analyses of Economic and Social Aspects of the Samurai in Tokugawa and Meiji Japan* (Harvard University Press, 1974).

Chapter 1—Norio Tamaki (see above); James L. McClain, "Space, Power, Wealth, and Status in Seventeenth-Century Osaka" and Tetsuo Najita, "Ambiguous Encounters: Ogata Kōan and International Studies in Late Tokugawa Osaka," both in

Osaka: The Merchants' Capital of Early Modern Japan, eds. James L. McClain and Wakita Osamu (Cornell University Press, 1999); Nobuhiko Nakai and James L. McClain, "Commercial Change and Urban Growth in Early Modern Japan" in The Cambridge History of Japan, Vol. 4, ed. John Whitney Hall (Cambridge University Press, 1991); Louis G. Perez, *Daily Life in Early Modern Japan* (Greenwood Press, 2002).

Chapter 2—John R. Black, *Young Japan: Yokohama and Yedo 1858-1870, Vol. 1 and 2*, (Oxford U. Press, 1968, reprint of 1883); W. G. Beasley, "The Foreign Threat and the Opening of the Ports" in *The Cambridge History of Japan Vol. 5*, ed. Marius B. Jansen (Cambridge University Press, 1989); W. G. Beasley, *Japan Encounters the Barbarian: Japanese Travellers in America and Europe* (Yale University Press, 1995); Andrew Cobbing, *The Japanese Discovery of Victorian Britain: Early Travel Encounters in the Far West* (Japan Library, 1998); Peter Booth Wiley, *Yankees in the Land of the Gods: Commodore Perry and the Opening of Japan* (Penguin Books, 1990); Samuel Eliot Morison, *"Old Bruin": Matthew Calbraith Perry*, (Atlantic Monthly Press, 1967); Walter LaFeber, *The Clash: U.S. Japanese Relations Throughout History* (W.W. Norton, 1997); Oliver Statler, *The Black Ship Scroll* (John Weatherhill Inc., 1963).

Chapter 3—Norio Tamaki (see above); James McClain, *A Modern History of Japan* (see above); *Fukuzawa Yûkichi On Education*, Kiyooka (see above); Marius B. Jansen "The Meiji Restoration" in *The Cambridge History of Japan Vol. 5*, ed. Marius B. Jansen (Cambridge University Press, 1989); W. G. Beasley, "Meiji Political Institutions" in *The Cambridge History of Japan, Vol. 5*, ed. Marius B. Jansen (Cambridge University Press, 1989); Hirakawa Sukehiro, "Japan's Turn to the West," trans. by Bob Tadashi Wakabayshi, in *The Cambridge History of Japan, Vol. 5*, ed. Marius B. Jansen (Cambridge University Press, 1989); David J. Lu, *Japan: A Documentary History*, Vol. II (M. E. Sharpe, 1997).

Chapter 4—James L. McClain, *A Modern History of Japan* (see above); William Reynolds Braister, trans. and intro., *Meiroku Zasshi: Journal of the Japanese Enlightenment* (Harvard University Press, 1976); Niculina Naw, "Concept Translation in Meiji Japan," *Translation Journal*, Vol. 3 #3 (July 1999); Hirakawa Sukehiro, "Japan's Turn to the West" (see above); Kenneth B. Pyle, "Meiji Conservatism," in *The Cambridge History of Japan, Vol. 5*, ed. Marius B. Jansen (Cambridge University Press, 1989); Albert M. Craig, "Fukuzawa Yūkichi: The Philosophical Foundations of Meiji Nationalism," *Political Development in Modern Japan*, ed. Robert E. Ward (Princeton University Press, 1968); Carmen Blacker (see above); *Fukuzawa Yūkichi, An Encouragement of Learning*, (see above); *Fukuzawa Yūkichi, An Outline of a Theory of Civilization* (see above); Yasukawa Jyunosuke, "Fukuzawa Yūkichi," *Ten Great Educators of Modern Japan: A Japanese Perspective*, ed. Benjamin Duke (University of Tokyo Press, 1989); Sharon L. Sievers, *Flowers in Salt: The Beginnings of a Feminist Consciousness in Modern Japan* (Stanford University Press, 1983); Earl H. Kinmouth, "Fukuzawa Reconsidered: Gakumon no Susume and Its Audience," in *Meiji Japan, Vol. II*, ed. Peter Kornicki (Routledge, 1998).

Chapter 5—Richard H. Mitchell, *Censorship in Imperial Japan* (Princeton University Press, 1983); Mikiso Hane, "Fukuzawa Yūkichi and Women's Rights," in *Meiji Japan, Vol II.*, ed. Peter Kornicki (Routledge Press, 1998); Sharon Sievers (see above); Daikichi Irokawa, *The Culture of the Meiji Period* (Princeton University Press, 1985); *Fukuzawa Yūkichi, An Outline of the Theory of Civilization* (see above); Michio Nagai, "Westernization and Japanization: The Early Meiji Transformation of Education," in *Tradition and Modernization of Japanese Culture*, ed. Donald H. Shively (Princeton University Press, 1971); Donald H. Shively, "The Japanization of the Middle Meiji," in *Tradition and Modernization of Japanese Culture*, ed. Donald H. Shively (Princeton University Press, 1971); Morikawa Terumichi, "Mori Arinori," *in Ten Great Educators of Modern Japan: A Japanese Perspective*, ed. Benjamin Duke (University of Tokyo Press, 1989).

Chapter 6—Mikiso Hane, "Fukuzawa Yūkichi and Women's Rights" (see above); Sharon Sievers (see above); Joyce Lebra, *Okuma Shigenobu: Statesman of Meiji Japan* (Australian National University Press, 1973); Yoshimitsu Khan, *Japanese Moral Education Past and Present* (Fairleigh Dickinson University Press, 1997); Fukuzawa Yûkichi on Japanese Women (see above); Fukuzawa Yûkichi: "An Outline of the Theory of Civilization" (see above); Fukuzawa Yûkichi on Education, trans. Kiyooka (see above); Michio Nagai (see above); Donald T. Roden, *Schooldays in Imperial Japan* (University of California Press, 1975); Morikawa Terumichi (see above); Ivan Parker Hall, *Mori Arinori* (Harvard University Press, 1973); James L. Huffman, *A Yankee in Meiji Japan: A Crusading Journalist, Edward H. House* (Rowman and Littlefield Publishers, 2003).

Chapter 7—Haru Matsukata Reischauer, *Samurai and Silk: A Japanese and American Heritage* (Harvard University Press, 1986); Norio Tamaki (see above); James L. McClain, *A Modern History of Japan* (see above); Joyce Lebra (see above); James L. Huffman, *Creating a Public: People and Press in Meiji Japan* (University of Hawaii Press, 1997); James L. Huffman, *Politics of the Meiji Press: The Life of Fukkuchi Gen'ichirô* (University of Hawaii Press, 1980); William De Lange, *A History of Japanese Journalism: Japan's Press Club As the Last Obstacle to a Mature Press* (Japan Library, 1998); In K. Hwang, *The Korean Reform Movement of the 1880s* (Shenkman Publishing Co., 1978); Miwa Kimitada, "Fukuzawa Yûkichi's 'Departure from Asia': A Prelude to the Sino-Japanese War," in *Japan's Modern Century*, ed. Edmund Skrzypczak (Sophia University Press, 1968); Carmen Blacker (see above); Stewart Lone, *Army Empire and Politics in Meiji Japan* (St. Martin's Press, 2000); Alan MacFarlane, *Fukuzawa and Maitland: The Making of the Modern World: Visions from the West and East* (Palgrave, 2001); Marius B. Jansen "Oi Kentaro: Radicalism and Chauvinism," *The Far Eastern Quarterly* (May 1952); Akira Iriye, "Japan Drives to Great Power Status" *in The Cambridge History of Japan, Vol. 5,* ed. Marius B. Jansen (Cambridge University Press, 1989); David J. Lu, trans. of Fukuzawa Yûkichi's "Goodbye Asia" (see above); Akira Iriye, *Japan & the Wider World: From the Mid-Nineteenth Century to the Present* (Longman, 1997).

Epilogue—Jyunosuke Yasukawa, "Fukuzawa Yûkichi" (see above); Lesley Downer, *Madame Sadayakko: The Geisha Who Seduced the West*, (Review, 2003); Tetsuo Najita, *Japan* (Prentice-Hall, 1974).

Glossary

Bakufu: central, military authority headed by the *shogun* and headquartered in Edo.

Bakufu **council:** a group of senior advisors to the *shogun*.

Castle town: urban centers that had sprung up around castles, where *samurai* were required by *bakufu* regulations to live.

Charter Oath: oath of five articles of 1868 which some believed promised a constitution and a governing assembly.

"Civilization and enlightenment:" *bunmei kaika*, slogan representing interest in western technology, science, and rational thought.

Class system: official *bakufu* system which established four primary classes in order from top to bottom *samurai*, peasant, artisan, merchant.

Confucianism: a Chinese import of moral and political thought which was selectively adapted by Japanese thinkers.

Constitutional Reform Party: *Rikken Seiyûkai*, moderate party.

Constitutional Imperial Party: *Rikken Teiseitô* conservative, pro-government party.

Council of State: three-pronged government established after 1868 that included legislative, executive, and judicial divisions to advise the emperor or, *de facto*, to run the government.

Daimyô: feudal lord, chief of a domain.

Deshima: manmade island off Nagasaki for Dutch traders.

Diet: Japanese parliament composed of a lower house (elected representatives) and upper house (members of the peerage).

Domain: *han* land given to a *daimyô* by Tokugawa central military authority, the *bakufu*.

Dutch studies: *rangaku*, education (particularly in science, technology, and medicine) through Dutch language texts.

Edo: old name for Tokyo.

Extraterritoriality: legal right given foreign nations to try their own citizens in their own courts for crimes committed in Japan.

Ezo: present-day island of Hokkaido.

Feudal system: codes governing relationships between the *bakufu* and *han* or the authorities in Edo and those in domains.

Freedom and popular rights movement: *jiyû minken*, political groups seeking governing role in the 1870s.

Fukoku kyôhei: "rich country strong army," slogan conveying aspirations of the new Meiji period rulers who wanted to compete with rich and strong western nations.

Furoshiki: cloth to wrap around small packages for carrying.

Geisha: high-class entertainer who sometimes became a mistress, a concubine, or a prostitute.

Geta: elevated wooden sandals which make it possible to walk across mud and through puddles.

Han: a domain governed by a *daimyô*.

Harris Treaty: "Treaty of Amity and Commerce Between the United States and Japan" negotiated by Townsend Harris in 1858.

Hatamoto: retainer or vassal of the *bakufu*.

Home Ministry: government bureau that promulgated harsh laws and housed the central police force that enforced laws censoring the press and speech as well as suppressing the right of citizens to assemble.

House of Peers: upper house of the Diet. Members were elected by other peers in their status group.

Imperial Court: traditional location of hereditary emperor's entourage.

Institute for the Study of Barbarian Books: *bakufu* center for study and translation of foreign learning.

Kanji: pictographs originally from Chinese which were used to write the Japanese language.

Keiô Gijuku **and University:** school and then university founded by Fukuzawa which continues today as one of Japan's elite private schools.

Koku: a measure of about 5 bushels.

Kuni no tame ni: "for the sake of the country," slogan encouraging citizens to work and fight for the nation's advancement.

Kurashiki: warehouse, storehouse.

Liberal Party: *Jiyûtô,* a radical party.

Lower House also known as the House of Representatives: formed in 1890 of a few men with property who could vote and hold office.

Lower-level samurai: the majority of *samurai* who received small stipends and had fewer privileges than upper level *samurai.*

Manifest destiny: belief that Americans were fated to claim all of the land between the original States and the Pacific Ocean.

Meiji Civil Law of 1898 also known as the Meiji Civil Code: included family laws which governed citizens lives and family relationships according to a Japanese version of the Confucian moral code.

Meiji Emperor: posthumous name for the emperor, Mutsuhito, who was placed in office in 1868 and reigned until his death in 1912.

Meiji Period: 1868-1912.

Meiji Six Society: *Meirokusha*, organization formed in the sixth year of Meiji by Fukuzawa and a few other educated and western oriented men.

"Most favored nation:" each foreign nation negotiating with Japan would receive same rights extended to any other nation.

Neo-Confucianism: revision of confucianism by Japanese scholars during the Tokugawa period which stressed orderly relationship between both human and natural worlds.

Oligarchs or oligarchy: a changing group of ex-*samurai* usually numbering about a dozen, mostly young, men who advised the Meiji emperor and in effect ran the government after 1868.

Peace Preservation Ordinance: (1887) signalled aggressive political war on freedoms of speech, assembly, publications.

Press laws: multiple laws of ever-increasing harshness calling for censorship and suppression of publication freedoms.

Regent to the *shogun*: underage *shogun's* advisor who, in reality, ran the shogunate.

***Rescript on Education*:** neo-Confucian statement in which citizens pledged allegiance to the state, the family system, the military, and the imperial system.

Restoration: *ôsei fukkô*, 1868 imperial restoration, the defeat of the *shogun* and the return of rule to the imperial court.

***Sakoku*:** "closed country" – policy of severely curtailing commerce between Japan and any foreign country.

***Samurai*:** highest of four basic classes within Tokugawa Japan representing the warrior tradition of earlier times.

***Sankin kôtai*:** *bakufu* law which required *daimyô* to spend every other year at their compound in Edo.

Sat-Chô: Satsuma and Chôshû domains.

***Sensei*:** teacher, term of honor for a superior.

***Shishi*:** "men of high purpose" who were anti-*bakufu* and pro-court.

Shogun: highest political and military position within the *bakufu* and, therefore, ruler from Edo during the Tokugawa period.

Sonnô jôi: "revere the emperor and expel the foreigner," slogan supporting the court and opposing foreign intrusion.

Stipend: amount of *samurai*'s income theoretically based on the amount of rice his allotment of land could produce.

Tatami: woven reed mats for floors with each mat being about 3 feet by 6 feet.

Terakoya: Tokugawa period temple schools.

Tokugawa: name of clan which defeated other clans in 1600 and therefore controlled the central shogunate until its defeat in 1868.

Treaty ports: ports in Japan in which foreigners could trade and live as established by commercial agreements.

Waseda University: *Semmon Gakkô* founded by Okuma Shigenobu in 1882. A private school which continues to compete with *Keiô* today.

Zaibatsu: financial, business, and manufacturing combines.

Index